AF564804

Policy Engagement and Extension

NIPA® GENX ELECTRONIC RESOURCES & SOLUTIONS P. LTD.
New Delhi-110 034

About the Authors

Preeti Tetarwal is a Ph.D. Scholar in the department of Agricultural Extension Education at Chaudhary Charan Singh Haryana Agricultural University, Hisar. She pursued her Master's degree from Navsari Agricultural University, Gujarat and Graduated from Swami Keshawanand Rajasthan Agricultural University, Bikaner, Rajasthan. In her credit, she has cleared ASRB NET in 2023 UGC NET in 2023 and 2024 and also secured UGC JRF in 2024. She has published a good number of research papers in NAAS rated journals. In her credit, she has many book chapters, popular articles.

P. Bhuvanasri is a Ph.D. Scholar in the department of Agricultural Extension Education at Chaudhury Charan Singh Haryana Agricultural University, Hisar. She has an experience of 3 years in research, extension and training in the discipline. She pursued her Master's degree from Central Agricultural University- Imphal and Graduated from Professor Jayashankar Telangana State Agricultural University, Hyderabad. In her credit, she has cleared UGC NET and ASRB NET in 2021 and 2023, secured UGC JRF in 2024.Her specialization is in Social Network Analysis and Climate smart Agriculture. She has published a good number of research papers in NAAS rated journals. In her credit, she has many book chapters, review papers popular articles, and is recipient of Best Oral and Poster presentation awards.

Saurabh Pandey is a Ph.D. student at Anand Agricultural University Anand, Gujarat in the department of Agricultural extension and communication. He received a master's degree from National Dairy Research Institute Karnal, Haryana. He graduated from Banda University of Agriculture and Technology, Banda, Uttar Pradesh. He has cleared ASRB NET in 2023 He has published many research papers, articles and book chapters and is a recipient of the best thesis award and best oral presentation award.

Dr. Jagannath Pathak is Professor & Head, Department of Soil Science & Agricultural Chemistry, College of Agriculture, Banda University of Agriculture &Technology, Banda. He has handled six international and national research projects relating to soil fertility and their management and Recipient of several awards including Bharat Gaurav award. He is working on restoration of soil fertility and nutrient management and delivering expert lectures on different aspects of agriculture. Dr. Pathak is a faculty of BUAT and actively engaged in teaching/ guiding of PG & Ph.D. students, research and extension in the area of Soil Science &Agricultural Chemistry. He has published more than 40 research papers and several book chapters, popular articles, leaflet/folders, technical bulletins and abstracts. He also delivered 30 radio and TV talks.

Policy Engagement and Extension

Preeti Tetarwal
Agricultural Extension Education
Chaudhary Charan Singh Haryana Agricultural University
Hisar, Haryana

Polasa Bhuvanasri
Agricultural Extension Education
Chaudhary Charan Singh Haryana Agricultural University
Hisar, Haryana

Saurabh Pandey
Agricultural Extension and Communication
Anand Agricultural University Anand, Gujarat

Jagannath Pathak
Department of Soil Science & Agricultural Chemistry
College of Agriculture
Banda University of Agriculture &Technology
Banda, Uttar Pradesh

NIPA® GENX ELECTRONIC RESOURCES & SOLUTIONS P. LTD.
New Delhi-110 034

**NIPA® GENX ELECTRONIC
RESOURCES & SOLUTIONS P. LTD.**

101,103, Vikas Surya Plaza, CU Block
L.S.C.Market, Pitam Pura, New Delhi-110 034
Ph : +91 11 4386 0225, 9717133558, 9540816132
E-mail: newindiapublishingagency@gmail.com
Website: www.niparesources.com

© 2025, Publisher

Print ISBN: 978-93-58877-33-5

ebook ISBN: 978-93-58873-17-7

All rights reserved. No part of this publication may be reproduced, stored in a retrieval system or transmitted in any form or by any means, including electronic, mechanical, photocopying recording or otherwise without the prior written permission of the publisher or the copyright holder.

This book contains information obtained from authentic and highly reliable sources. Reasonable efforts have been made to publish reliable data and information, but the author/s, editor/s and publisher cannot assume responsibility for the validity, accuracy or completeness of all materials or information published herein or the consequences of their use. The work is published with the understanding that the publisher and author/s are not attempting to render any professional services. The author/s, editor/s and publisher have attempted to trace and acknowledge the copyright holders of all material reproduced in this publication and apologize to copyright holders if permission and/or acknowledgements to publish in this form have not been taken. If any copyrighted material has not been acknowledged, please write to us and let us know so that we may rectify the error, in subsequent reprints.

Trademark Notice: NIPA®, the NIPA® logos and their presentations (the way they are written/ presented) in this book are the trademarks of the publisher and hence may not be used without written permission, if copied or used without authorization, the infringer will be prosecuted as per law.

NIPA® also publishes books in a variety of electronic formats. Some content that appears in print may not be available in electronic books, and vice versa

Composed and Designed by NIPA®.

Preface

The BSMA Committee report submitted by the Indian Council of Agricultural Research (ICAR) are developed to streamline and address postgraduate and PhD programs. On the recommendations of the NCG, 19 Broad Subject Matter Area (BSMA) Committees have been constituted by the ICAR for revising the syllabus. These Committees held discussions at length in the meetings and workshops organized across the country, framed and revised the content.

Core areas like understanding the policy, importance of policies for extension, ensure funding, institutional restructuring, capacity building of extension functionaries, types of policies, policy as a product and process, structured policies and institutions-how this influence defining organizational roles and performance in extension organizations, formulation of policies, role and importance of policies in up scaling knowledge, role of governments support policies in knowledge-based institutions success. policy advocacy and tools, approaches to policy advocacy, policy advocacy strategies, policy analysis, types of policy analysis, have been described with suitable illustrations in simple understandable language for the readers. methods and techniques commonly used in policy analysis, ethical policy analysis, tools for policy impact research, policy influence tools, policy development process, environmental factors, environmental factors, influencing policy change through generating evidence, engaging with policymakers, global experience with agricultural extension policies, challenges in policy implementation etc., all the above mentioned topics were well documented according to the syllabus.

An attempt has been made to include newer areas and concepts according to guidelines of Broad Subject Matter Area Committees (BSMA) for the benefit of the readers. This book tried to incorporate the recent advances. We acknowledge the authors whose study has been cited and to all those who motivated us to bring out this publication. We also acknowledge sincere efforts of reviewers in compilation and publication of the book.

Authors

Acknowledgement

First and foremost, I offer my deepest gratitude to God, whose grace and strength have sustained me throughout this journey. Without his blessings, this hardcover would not have been possible.

I am profoundly grateful to the professors, whose invaluable advice and support have been instrumental in the development of this work. Your wisdom, encouragement, and constructive feedback have guided me through every stage of this process.

I would also like to express heartfelt thanks to my family, whose love and support have been my bedrock. Special thanks to parents for your unwavering belief in me, and for your patience and understanding throughout the writing of this book.

My sincere appreciation extends to my friends and colleagues, whose insights and camaraderie have enriched both my life and this work. Your encouragement and suggestions have helped shape this project into what it is today.

Finally, to all the readers and contributors who have played a role, your interest and feedback have been a source of motivation. Acknowledging each and everyone for being part of this journey.

Authors

Contents

1

Understanding Policy

Importance of Policies for Extension

Policies play an important role in the field of extension, which involves the transfer ofknowledge and technology from researcher to farmers, communities and other stakeholders. Following are some specific reasons why policies are vital for extension:

1. **Accountability:** Policies may provide basis for monitoring and evaluation of extension activities and for holding extension professionals and other stakeholders accountable for their actions.
2. **Innovation:** Policies can promote innovation in extension by encouraging the adoption of new technology, approaches and practices, encouraging experimentation, collaboration and continuous improvement. By removing barriers to adoption and offering rewards for testing, policies can also aid in the creation of an atmosphere that fosters innovation.
3. **Consistency:** Policies aid in ensuring that extension activities are consistent with the goals and objectives of organization or program. It offers a framework for decision-making that enables the uniform handling of similar circumstances.
4. **Effectiveness:** Policies guarantee that extension initiatives are successful in producing the desired results. Policies aid in ensuring that extension operations are concentrated on producing the desired effects by providing a framework for behaviour and decision-making.
5. **Transparency:** Policies aid in ensuring the fairness and transparency of extension activities. When policies are in place, those who are participating in extension efforts are aware of what is expected of them and the implications of their decision.
6. **Resource allocation:** Policies help governments and organizations allocate resources effectively to support agricultural extension services. They ensure that funding, human resources and infrastructure are available to deliver extension programs to farmers.

7. **Coordination:** Policies provide a framework for coordinating various stakeholders involved in agricultural extension, including government agencies, non-governmental organizations, research institutions and farmers' groups. This coordination ensures that extension services are delivered efficiently and without duplication.
8. **Quality control:** Policies can establish standards and guidelines for the quality of extension services, including the training and qualifications of extension workers. This helps maintain the credibility and effectiveness of the extension system.
9. **Targeting:** Policies can help identify priority areas and target specific groups of farmers who need extension services the most. For example, policies can prioritize support for smallholder farmers, women, or marginalized communities.
10. **Technology adoption:** Policies can promote the adoption of modern agricultural technologies, practices and innovations. They can create incentives for farmers to embrace new techniques that can improve their yields, reduce losses and enhance sustainability.
11. **Market access:** Extension policies in Agricultural Sciences can help farmers access markets by providing information on market opportunities, price trends and value-added processing. This can increase farmers' incomes and overall economic development in rural areas.
12. **Data collection and analysis:** Policies can mandate the collection of agricultural data and support research to generate knowledge about local farming conditions. This information is crucial for tailoring extension services to the specific needs of different regions and crops.
13. **Capacity building:** Extension policies can support the training and professional development of extension workers, ensuring that they have the necessary skills and knowledge to assist farmers effectively.
14. **Feedback mechanisms:** Policies can establish mechanisms for feedback and communication between extension providers and farmers. This allows for continuous improvement and adjustment of extension services based on farmers' needs and feedback.

Overall, policies are imperative in extension because they help in ensuring that extension programs are approachable to the needs of society and stakeholders and that they are designed and implemented in a way that maximizes their impact and effectiveness. They also provide a mechanism for engaging stakeholders in the extension process and fostering approaches.

Role of Policy in Providing Structure

Policies help to structure extension programme by specifying the duties and responsibilities of various stakeholders such as extension workers, administrators and clients. They serve to provide a clear and consistent approach to extension work by establishing the organized work structure, governance arrangements and operating procedures of extension organizations.

Policies play a key role in providing structure to agricultural extension systems. They establish the framework within which extension services operate, guiding the activities, objectives and organization of extension programs.

- **Clear objectives:** Policies define the overarching goals and objectives of agricultural extension programs. They specify what the extension system aims to achieve, such as increasing crop yields, improving livestock management, enhancing food security, or promoting sustainable farming practices.
- **Scope and coverage:** Policies outline the scope of extension services and the target audience. They define which agricultural sectors or commodities are covered, as well as the geographic areas or communities that will receive extension support.
- **Institutional structure:** Policies establish the institutional framework for delivering extension services. They define the roles and responsibilities of government agencies, research institutions non-governmental organizations and other stakeholders involved in extension.
- **Funding and resources:** Policies allocate financial resources and other necessary resources to support extension programs. They specify budgetary allocations, funding sources and mechanisms for resource mobilization.
- **Quality standards:** Policies set quality standards and guidelines for extension services. They define the qualifications and training requirements for extension workers, ensuring that they have the necessary expertise to deliver effective support to farmers.
- **Monitoring and evaluation:** Policies establish mechanisms for monitoring and evaluating the performance of extension programs. They define key performance indicators, data collection methods and reporting requirements.
- **Adaptability:** Policies should allow for adaptability to changing circumstances and emerging challenges in agriculture. They may include mechanisms for periodic policy review and updates to ensure that extension services remain relevant and effective.

Ensure Funding

The most difficult and challenging policy issue facing extension today is to secure a stable source of funding. With the widespread trend to cut government budgets, including structural adjustment programmes, many policy makers have the impression that public extension is both expensive and a drain on the government's limited resources.

The issue of funding extension continues to be the most difficult policy issue faced by extension. This issue is complicated by the increased demand for more extension services on the part of increasing numbers of farm households who have fewer land and water resources. Furthermore, extension is being called to integrate sustain-able development messages into its extension programmes. This results in "working with less to do more."

a. Collaborate to develop, establish and operate a stakeholder-driven trust fund
b. managed by a board of trustees, to finance pluralistic extension services.
c. A competitive grant system will be used by private sector and public institutions including universities to access extension funds.
d. Empower extension clientele through promoting diversification of enterprises.
e. Decentralize the extension service delivery system and use cost-effective approaches and methodologies

Policy Framework for Providing Functions

Transformations in agricultural extension already initiated and proposed to be undertaken on wider scale are discussed under the following sub-heads:

- Policy reforms
- Institutional restructuring
- Management reforms
- Strengthening Research –Extension linkages
- Capacity building and skill upgradation
- Empowerment of farmers
- Mainstreaming of women in Agriculture
- Use of media & information technology
- Financial sustainability
- Changing role of government

Policy Reforms

Farming systems approach- Reforms in Agricultural Extension envisage the addition of the old single-discipline based, commodity-oriented approach of the T & V system by the Farming Systems (FS) approach. The FS approach considers the farm, household and off-farm activities in all-inclusive way to take care not only of farming but also all facets of nutrition, food security, sustainability, risk minimization, income and employment generation which make up the several objectives of farm households. The FS approach emphasizes that research and extension agendas should be determined by explicitly defined farmers' needs through an understanding of the existing farming systems rather than perceptions by research scientists or extension functionaries.

Multi-agency extension service- For many years agricultural extension was considered the monopoly of the public sector. However, with the wide range of demands for agricultural technology in the changing scenario there is growing recognition that public extension by itself cannot meet the specific needs of various regions and different classes of farmers.

The three arms of the agricultural extension network are:

1. Public extension services
2. Private extension services
3. Mass media services

1. Public Extension Services

a. State government line departments operated extension (Departments of Agriculture, Horticulture & Livestock development)
b. State agriculture universities-based extension (Directorates of Extension, Krishi Vigyan Kendras (KVKs) and Krishi Gyan Kendras (KGKs)
c. ICAR extension (Zonal Research Stations/ Krishi Vigyan Kendras)
d. Agriculture Technology Information Centres (ATICs), Institute Village Linkage Programme (IVLP) *etc.*,

2. Private Extension Services

a. Community Based (Farmers' Organizations, Farmers' Cooperatives, Self Help Groups *etc.*)
b. Para Extension Workers (contact farmers, link farmers, g*opals, mitra kisans, mahila mitra kisans, etc.*)
c. Agri-Clinics & Agribusinesses

d. Input Suppliers/ Dealers (Pesticides, Seeds, Nutrients, Farm Implements, *etc.*

e. Corporate Sector (Commercial Crops – tobacco, tea, coffee, oilseeds (sunflower), vegetables, Seeds, Farm Implements – tractors, threshers, sprinklers, drip irrigation, *etc.*)

3. Mass Media

a. The mass are approached through films, slides, radio talks, mews paper, circular letters, television, poster *etc.* and provide helpful repetition for those contacted personally or through groups.

b. Mass media enables extension workers to improve their teaching efficiency.

c. This facilitates dissemination of information to a much larger group of people.

d. Farm Publications, Circular letters, News Articles, Radio, Television *etc.*,

Institutional Restructuring

It is clear that no one uniform extension system will serve as a solution to every system. Even within States there will be a combination of various agencies and different institutional arrangements to address the needs of differing agro-climatic zones as well as different sections of farmers. A set menu of various models will be available to the States to select and adapt to their own requirements.

Restructuring Public Extension

Public extension will continue to remain central to technology dissemination, small , marginal farmers and economically backward regions will need to be serviced by it. This implies that public extension functionaries (including VEWs & SMSs) will have to be placed in new decentralized institutional arrangements which are demand-driven, farmer-accountable, bottom-up and have a Farming Systems Approach (broad-based).

District Level Agriculture Technology Management Agency (ATMA) model

The key concept is to ***decentralized decision-making*** at the district level through the creation of the ATMA as a registered society. A second goal is to increase farmer input into program planning and resource allocation, especially at the block level to be accountable to stakeholders. A third major goal is to increase program coordination and integration between departments so that the following program thrusts can be more effectively and efficiently implemented.

Farming System Innovations— Includes the intensification and/or diversification into high value commodities, value-added marketing and processing activities

Farmer organizations—are specially for high value commodities and resource poor farmers,

Bridging technology gaps in both crop and livestock production systems

Natural Resource Management—specifically soil and water management to reduce pesticide use through Integrated Pest Management (IPM) programmes.

Marketing and agro-processing linkages between farmers' groups, markets and private processor.

Strategic Research and Extension Plans (SREPs) Through Participatory Rural Appraisal (PRA)

In the process of creating a more bottom-up extension system, PRA procedures would be familiarized across all system levels (district, block, mandal and village) and across each participating line department (DOA, DOH, DAH and Department of Marketing) and research institutions (ZRS and KVKs) within the district. On the basis of PRA, Strategic Research Extension Plans would be organized for the districts. The district SREP must be grounded at the block or mandal level, where extension programs can be fine-tuned to the requirements of farmers and more effectively implemented. The SREP would take account of the research, training and extension requirements for production as well as marketing activities.

Refining Eesearch-extension Linkages

Promotion of direct interface between farmers and scientists- The direct interface between scientists and farmers is the most idyllic and should be undertaken wherever possible. It is an oft- repeated process that farmers learn best from scientists or other successful farmers. Moreover, transmission losses are lessened in the direct interface.

Activating existing interface mechanisms- Regional committees of the ICAR, zonal interfaces initiated by DAC, national level pre-kharif and pre-rabi DAC-ICAR interface, state level bi-annual meetings between line departments and SAUs are all formally instituted mechanisms for improving research-extension linkages. Several of these mechanisms have fallen into disuse or are conducted in a perfunctory manner. As a result, the desired results are not being achieved. These will be activated.

Research priority setting based on SREP- Micro-level extension strategies reflected in the Strategic Research and Extension Plans (SREPs) grounded on PRA and developed jointly by the district technology teams (DTTs) together with the marketing department officials and scientists of the KVKs/ ZRS or SAUs should get formal feedback into the research systems through a research priority setting mechanism in the ICAR.

Capacity Building of Extension Functionaries

One-time grant for training infrastructure- One-shot up-gradation of physical infrastructure of training institutes/ centres be considered to revive the training institutes to an acceptable level. Funding for this purpose to be made jointly by the central and State governments.

Upgrading state level extension management training institutions

Strengthening role of MANAGE. The National Institute of Agricultural Extension Management (MANAGE) will be strengthened to enable it to assist the States in developing their HRD capacities.

Developing Professionalism in Cost Effective Manner

Training institutes/ centres may focus on developing core competency; other services may be out-sourced or contracted. Feedback from participants must be used to evaluate performance of faculty

Training institutes and SAUs: To train private extension functionaries. Facilities of public training institutions and SAUs would be available to NGOs and private extension agents.

Networking Among all State Level Institutes

All national and state level training institutes will be networked to state headquarters, SAUs and MANAGE. The network will also include private institutions with expertise in different fields.

Empowerment of Farmers

Linking farmers in setting extension agenda. Farmers' representation as major stakeholders will be ensured in all decision -making bodies of public and private extension services. Farmer will be involved in the planning and implementation of extension programmes through formal institutional mechanisms such as ATMAs, FACs *etc.*

Implementation of programmes through Farmers' User Groups. By ensuring that all programmes in the field are planned and implemented through farmer user groups, such as Watershed Associations, fruit/vegetable growers societies, Agricultural Produce Marketing Societies/ Cooperatives *etc.,* farmers would be able to impact both administrative and financial decisions. Stringent arrangements between governments, extension services and farmers, whereby the farmers could play the role of beneficiaries, provider or co-financier of extension services.

1. Assessing farmers' needs and skills;
2. Unique dimensions of training such in creating awareness, knowledge, skills and reinforcement and via appropriate channels and methods for each;
3. Different kinds of technologies and advice required by different categories of male and female farmers, the transfer mechanism (*e.g.* direct, mass media, different types of groups) they prefer during different phases of awareness, trial and adoption of new skills and technologies
4. Usage of information technology for improving the quality and accelerating the transfer and exchange of information
5. Organizing training programmes on system based and sustainable technologies such as Integrated Pest Management (IPM) and Integrated Plant Nutrient management (IPNM);

Arranging training and taking initiatives for capacity building of farmers towards agricultural marketing. Capacity building, skill up gradation/training of farmers would be largely conducted through farmers' field schools with an active participation of scientists and extension personnel.

Mainstreaming Women in Agriculture

Gender concerns need to be mainstreamed in the agricultural extension process. Extension systems provided by Government which must disseminate new technology and information, are still largely male highlighted. Hence the necessity to target women is to ensure that they receive information relevant to their effort, predominantly with preference to crops and livestock.

Growing the Sphere of Women Extension Workers

The number of female agricultural extension workers would be increased through

(i) Re-examination of all service cadre rules for hidden gender biases
(ii) Improvement of female attendance at agricultural institutes and school
(iii) Building incentives such as scholarships and stipends for more women to take up under- graduate and post graduate courses in the agricultural and allied sciences
(iv) Redesigning of agricultural training curricula to include women's concerns:
(v) Ensuring that women are adequately represented in all training programmes whether domestic or overseas
(vi) Redesigning of training facilities to make them suitable for large numbers of female students and trainees;
(vii) Attachment of teaching curricula for extension workers, bigger analysis and extension methods that take into account women's time, mobility and cultural condition; and
(viii) Exploring the specific role of farm women in the marketing of agricultural produce.

Policy: Definition and Types

"A set of ideas or a plan of what to do in particular situations that has been agreed to officially by a group of people, a business organization, a government, or a political party"

"A definite course or method of action selected from among alternatives and in light of given conditions to guide and determine present and future decisions; a high-level overall plan embracing the general goals and acceptable procedures especially of a governmental body"

Policy refers to a set of principles, guidelines, or rules that are formulated and implemented by organizations, governments, or institutions to achieve specific goals or objectives. Policies are often designed to address various issues, ranging from social, economic and political matters to organizational management and governance.

Extension Policy

Extension policy specifically Agricultural Extension is a part of national development policy in general and of agricultural and rural development policy in particular. Hence, agricultural extension is one of the policy instruments which governments can use to stimulate agricultural development.

Categories of Policies

American political scientist Theodore J. Lowi proposed four types of policy: in his article *"Four Systems of Policy, Politics* and *Choice"* and *in "American Business, Public Policy, Case Studies* and *Political Theory*"

a. Distributive
b. Regulatory
c. Redistributive and
d. Constituent

a. **Distributive policies:** It extends goods and services to members of an organization, as well as distributing the costs of the goods/services amongst the members of the organization.

   Example: Government policies that impact spending for welfare, public education, highways and public safety, or a professional organization's benefits plan.

b. **Regulatory policies**: It limits the discretion of individuals and agencies, or otherwise compel certain types of behaviour. These policies are applied when good behaviour can be easily defined and bad behaviour can be easily regulated.

   Example: Highway speed limit.

c. **Redistributive policies:** Policies are dynamic; they are not just static lists of goals or laws. Policy blueprints have to be implemented, often with unexpected results. Social policies are what happens 'on the ground' when they are implemented

   Example: The equal opportunity policy of a company shows that the company aims to treat all its staff equally.

d. **Constituent policies** create executive power entities or deal with laws. Constituent policies also deal with fiscal policy in some circumstances.

Some other Policies Designed by

Public

Public Policy generally determines the lines along which human beings in a particular country can operate. Policy impacts everything from the legality of activities, to voting and even which side of the road you can drive your vehicle

Organizational

Internal and external stakeholders of a specific organization make this type of policy. It is the type of policy that aims at deciding the goals and activities of the entire organization. Policies of this sort usually anchor on the co-values of the organization and what purpose it serves. Non-Governmental Organization (NGO) that advocates for human rights. They can develop a policy that makes sure these are respected starting from within the NGO before being extended to the field. Such organizations create codes of conduct that are characterized by criticism against, discrimination along racial or tribal lines.

Functional

Companies among other organizations are organized into departments that have different functions. These Units and divisions necessitated this type of policy. These are assigned to specific areas in any kind of setup. These range from financial, production, marketing and others.

You may then find that separate departments in the same organization have policies that only apply to one but not the other. However, these policies should never be conflicting. In order to achieve organizational goals, there is a necessity to harmonize departmental policies.

Specific

Be it in the government or the private sector, this type of policy is formulated to address a particular issue and usually is temporary

Example: How Covid-19 has impacted policymaking in your respective country. Activities of the old day being banned and in some instances referred to as illegal and attracting fines and even jail penalties. Not only public policy was affected, but private entities are also changing their policies to suit the new business atmosphere.

Based on the Level of Formation

a) **Top management policies**: created by the higher executives such as the Managing Director, Vice-Chancellor and General Manager.

   Ex: investments, diversification, acquisitions, available capital

b) **Middle-level management policies**: developed after discussions between middle and upper-level executives. Ex: employee selection for a specific job, installation of new equipment

c) **Lower-level management policies**: developed by supervisors who are in charge of providing tools, raw materials, training, quality control, discipline, improving employee morale and reducing absenteeism, among other things. They are directly involved in achieving the organization's goals

d) **Operational-level management policies**: are written down in manuals and workbooks that the operational-level employees are expected to follow.

1. Prescribed: Formulated by the top management based on the company's objectives and employees are expected to comply with them.

a) **Suggested**: "Proposed policies", based on employee suggestions or input from consultants. They are often more effective as they involve employee participation and can help build buy-in.

b) **Compulsory:** Not willingly accepted by employees but are enforced by external forces such as government regulations, trade unions, legal acts and societal norms. Employees must follow these policies, whether they agree with them or not.

c) **Derived**: Developed by departments or sections based on the major or basic policies. They serve as operational guidelines for day-to-day activities.

2. Managerial Function-based Policies

a) **Planning:** For organizational management as they provide direction and help achieve company objectives. Involve collecting information, developing alternate courses of action and determining the best course of action.

b) **Organizing:** To function efficiently - establishing and maintaining a clear and precise organizational structure, determining the role of each level of management, deciding the level of authority,

c) **Directional:** Vital for accomplishing organizational goals by providing effective leadership and guiding individuals towards success through suitable tasks and communication.

d) **Controlling:** For measuring organizational performance, involving continuous observation of results against pre-established standards, identifying deviations and taking corrective action.

3. Situational or Contingency Policies

Organizations formulate these policies on an ad-hoc basis in response to specific situations or events that require a unique or customized solution. Organizations revise these policies according to changes in the situation and modify them as needed since they are not static and remain flexible.

a) **Contingency:** crisis management policies, disaster management policies, risk management policies.

b) **Environmental policies:** These policies outline an organization's commitment to environmental sustainability and responsible business practices, such as reducing waste and minimizing carbon emissions.

c) **Ethical policies:** These policies outline an organization's code of ethics and standards for ethical behaviour

Other Types of Policy

A. Domestic policy

Domestic policy is an area of public policy which concerns, laws, government programs and administrative decisions which are directly interrelated to all issues and activity within a nation's borders. It differs from foreign policy, which refers to the ways a government advances its interests in world politics.

B. Foreign policy

A country's foreign policy, also called the foreign relations policy, consists of self-interest strategies chosen by the state to safeguard its national interests and to achieve its goals within international relations milieu. The approaches are strategically employed to interact with other countries.

There are different ways to look at policy

C. Vertical and Horizontal Policy

Vertical policy is developed within a single organizational structure and generally starts with broad overarching policy, sometimes called "corporate" or "framework" policy. Such decisions are made at head office and guide subsequent decisions throughout the organization. At the regional level we might develop regional or "strategic" policy, which translates the national decisions to the regional level, taking into consideration the specific context. Finally, the regional policy is made specific enough to guide operational decision-making.

Horizontal policy- is developed by two or more organizations, each of which has the ability or mandate to deal with only one dimension of a given situation. Horizontal or integrated policy is created between parts of an organization or among organizational components that are similar in hierarchical position. Governments increasingly are focusing their efforts upon horizontal policymaking in recognition of the fact that many of the objectives they seek to achieve are complex and relate to the mandates of two or more departments, jurisdictions or non-governmental organizations. Areas of common interest include, for example, climate change, Aboriginal issues and the range of concerns rooted in cities and communities.

D. Reactive and proactive policy

Policy can also be categorized as reactive and proactive.

a. **Reactive policy:** It emerges in response to a concern or crisis that must be addressed – health emergencies and environmental disasters are two examples.
b. **Proactive policies:** By contrast, are introduced and pursued through deliberate choice. The national skills and learning agenda exemplify this approach. Knowledge and learning increasingly have been recognized as vital keys that unlock the doors to both economic wealth and social well-being.

E. Current and Future Policy

a. **Current policy:** There is another way to categorize various policies: those that are currently on the public agenda and those that are not. Current policy: Issues already on the public policy agenda (e.g., health care) often have high profile. A formal process to amend or improve the existing arrangement generally is in place.
b. **Future policy:** If an issue is not currently or never has been 'alive' on the public agenda, then there is work to be done in making the case for its importance and raising awareness about the implications of non-response.

F. Social Policy

This research investigates how policies affect individuals, groups and communities with the goal of identifying the most effective policies for addressing social issues and advancing social justice.

International: Social policy specifically discusses social and governmental issues from both the viewpoints of developed welfare systems and those of developing nations. The various public policy actor configurations (state, family, market and civil society) involved in delivering social welfare in various situations are given careful consideration.

Interdisciplinary: The approach to social and public policy encompasses a wide-ranging multidisciplinary study of the circumstances, institutions and forces that shape social change, relying on viewpoints from anthropology, criminology, demography, economics, political science, sociology and development.

G. Applied: In a wide range of subject areas and in high-, middle- and low-income country contexts, social policy emphasizes the analytical and conceptual skills required for probing social problems, analyzing how social policies are implemented and evaluating the (positive and negative) consequences of those policies

Is Policy a Product or a Process or Both?

Policy can be both a product and a process, depending on how you view it and the context in which it is considered.

Policy as a Product

Outcome or Document

In one sense, a policy is a product because it results in a tangible document or outcome. It's a formal statement or set of guidelines that outlines a course of action, rules or principles to be followed. This document is the end result of the policymaking process.

For example, a government's environmental policy document outlines its stance on environmental protection, including specific regulations and initiatives to achieve its environmental goals.

Policy as a Process

Decision-making process: Policy can also be viewed as a process, which encompasses the entire lifecycle of policymaking. This process involves several stages, including problem identification, policy formulation, decision-making, implementation and evaluation.

For example, the process of developing an environmental policy involves identifying environmental issues, researching potential solutions, consulting stakeholders, making decisions on specific measures, implementing those measures and continually evaluating their effectiveness. The distinction between policy as a product and policy as a process highlights that policies are not static; they evolve and adapt over time. The policymaking process is dynamic and involves ongoing revisions, adjustments and evaluations of policy outcomes. The policy document itself is the formalized representation of decisions made within this process

Policies and Institutions- How this Influence Defining Organizational Roles and Performance in Extension Organizations

1. **Centralized organization:** Department of Agricultural Extension in Thailand and Bangladesh, the Agricultural Extension Bureau of South Korea and AGRITEX in Zimbabwe. This form of organization includes the national extension office manages and controls extension programme activities and resources at the regional, district, sub district and village level. Clientele participation and feedback in programme planning are generally limited.
2. **Decentralized organization**: Examples of this form of extension organization are the agricultural extension systems in Brazil, Canada, India, Nigeria and the Philippines. These systems have almost an invisible national or federal extension office, in that extension programming, management and the control of activities and resources are vested with state or provincial governments.
3. **Cooperative type of extension organization and funding:** The distinguishing feature of this form of extension organization is the cooperation or partnership between the national, state or provincial and local governments in funding, programming and managing the activities and resources of extension. In the United States, extension is a joint undertaking of the U.S. Department of Agriculture (Federal Extension Service), the state land-grant universities and the county governments.
4. **Pluralistic forms of a national extension system:** This is an emerging form of extension organization in many countries, but it is not yet reflected in national extension policy. This structure appears to occur in those countries where the need for extension services is widespread and/or where the public agricultural extension organization can no longer satisfy its clientele because of resource and management problems. As a consequence, many publicly and/or privately funded organizations, including Non-Governmental Organizations (NGOs), are beginning to conduct agricultural extension programmes. Publicly funded extension organizations may include the crop, livestock and horticulture departments of the ministry of agriculture, state-funded agricultural colleges, universities along with commodity boards. Privately funded organizations may include rural development-oriented NGOs, agrobusiness firms (contract extension) and farmer organizations, including cooperatives and commodity associations. Generally, the geographical, subject-matter and clientele coverage and the standard of work for each of these different organizations are not known. Also, these separate efforts are generally not well coordinated.

Formulation of Policies

They are mainly in four different ways:

a. May be originated by management.
b. Through appeal.
c. May be implied from the decisions and actions of the company's executives.
d. Can be externally imposed.

a. **May be originated by management:** Managers originate policies to ensure that decisions within the organization will be in line with its objectives. Generally, they are written and embodied in the company's policy manual, if it has one.

b. **Through appeal:** A situation develops where an executive is uncertain whether he or she has the authority to make a decision. Consequently, he or she appeals to higher-level management for the decision. Once the decision is made, it becomes precedent for similar decisions in the future. A set of unwritten, incomplete and uncoordinated policies may emerge.

c. **May be implied from the decisions and actions of the company's executives:** Not uncommon to find that some of the "real" policies of a company differ from its stated policies. For example, a company may have a stated policy of promoting strictly on the basis of merit whereas in reality, relatives and personal friends of top management are given priority.

d. **Can be externally imposed:** Not infrequently, outside institutions, such as various departments of government, trade unions and trade associations, impose requirements on organizations. Labor contracts and federal regulations are familiar examples. Consider how the equal opportunity employment laws have led to major modifications in the personnel policies of many firms.

Hierarchal Structure of Policies

a. Found in all levels of organizations
b. At the very top, key policies may be important elements of the company's overall strategy and help define how it differentiates itself from its rivals and competes in the marketplace.
c. Such policies are generally called functional strategies because they guide strategic decision making at the functional level

d. High-level policies typically must be interpreted and narrowed at lower organizational levels.
e. Results in a hierarchical structure of policies within organizations.
f. Policies tend to be broad at higher organizational levels and become successively more restrictive as they move down the hierarchy.
g. To elaborate, a company might have a functional strategy of aggressive price competition.
h. At the sales manager level, this policy might be refined to state that the company will meet competitors' prices on all of the firm's non-proprietary products.
i. And, at the district level, the policy might be narrowed again to read that district sales managers can make price concessions up to (10%) on their own authority but, beyond that, they must get approval from above.

Role of Policies in Upscaling Knowledge

National extension systems can follow several different extension approaches in implementing extension policy. Most extension systems in developing countries give primary attention to technology transfer, given national agricultural policies that emphasize increasing food production and achieving national food security. An example of a technology transfer approach would be the Training and Visit (T&V) Extension System that has been promoted by the World Bank through its lending programme.

Knowledge

a. Knowledge is an organized set of statement of fact or ideas, presenting a reasoned judgment or an experimental result, which is transmitted to others through some communication medium in some systematic form.
b. Knowledge consists of new judgments (Research and Scholarship) or presentation of older judgments as exemplified in text books, teaching and learning and collected as library and archival material.
c. Knowledge is a fluid mix of framed experience, values, contextual information and expert insight that provides an environment and framework for evaluating and incorporating new experiences and information.
d. Knowledge is a highly organized intellectual product of humans that includes personal experience, skills, understanding of the different contexts in which we operate our activities, assimilation of all these and recording all this in a form that could be communicated to others.

Scaling up Knowledge Through

a. Research institutions and laboratories
b. Research and development establishments
c. Universities and professional institutions
d. Institutions of higher learning
e. Learned societies and professional associations
f. Government ministries, departments
g. Industries and business houses

Role of Governments' Support Policies in Knowledge-Based Institutions Success

1. **Education and skill development:** Policies can promote and prioritize investments in education sector and skill development sector, ensuring that individuals have access to quality learning opportunities throughout their lives. This includes policies that support early childhood education, primary and secondary education, vocational training, higher education and lifelong learning programs. By enhancing the educational infrastructure and curriculum, policies can foster the acquisition and upscaling of knowledge.
2. **Research and development:** Policies can encourage and support Research and Development (R&D) activities across various sectors. Governments can allocate funds for research grants, establish research institutes and centers of excellence and incentivize private sector investments in R&D through tax breaks or other means. Such policies stimulate innovation, generate new knowledge and facilitate its application in practical settings.
3. **Open Access and Knowledge Sharing:** Policies that promote open access to knowledge can significantly contribute to upscaling knowledge. Governments and institutions can implement open access mandates, requiring publicly funded research to be freely available to the public.

   Additionally, policies can support the development of Open Educational Resources (OER) and open-source software, enabling wider access to educational materials and fostering collaborative knowledge creation and sharing.
4. **Intellectual Property protection:** Effective Intellectual Property (IP) policies, including copyright, patents and trademarks, can incentivize knowledge creation and dissemination. By providing legal protection and

economic incentives to inventors, innovators and creators, these policies encourage the sharing of knowledge and technological advancements.

5. **Digital infrastructure and connectivity:** Policies that focus on improving digital infrastructure and connectivity, such as broadband internet access, can expand access to knowledge and information.

   By reducing the digital divide, these policies enable individuals and communities to participate fully in the digital age, access online educational resources and engage in knowledge-sharing platforms.

6. **Collaboration and partnerships:** Policies can facilitate collaboration and partnerships among various stakeholders, including government, academia, industry and civil society. Such policies can establish platforms for knowledge exchange, joint research initiatives and collaborative problem-solving. By fostering cooperation and leveraging diverse expertise, these policies accelerate the upscaling of knowledge

2

Policy Advocacy and Tools

Definition of advocacy, approaches to policy advocacy-advising, media campaigning, lobbying, Activism, Information Education Communication (IEC) and Behavior Change Communication (BCC), Advocacy for Rural Advisory Services (RAS), Policy advocacy strategy

Introduction

The word "Advocacy" is defined as any action that promotes, urges, justifies defends, or pleads on behalf of another person is referred to as advocacy.

In all its manifestations, advocacy works to make sure that people, especially those who are most sure people, especially those who are most at risk in a group or society can:

- Have their opinions taken into account when decisions about their lives are being made
- Speak up for matters that are important to them.
- Defend and protect their rights
- Have their voice heard on key subjects.

For instance, many undergraduate students believed that using government funding for research constituted advocacy. Undergraduates and NGO professionals were more likely to concur on what advocacy entailed, including a broad range of activities under the term "advocacy" including presenting science at public events and serving in an advisory capacity for a scientific society, as well as even giving presentations at conferences or publishing peer-reviewed papers. On the other side, government officials and academics shared a similar mentality and has a more constrained understanding of what lobbying involved, emphasizing activities like writing to congress about a policy or providing advice to a special interest group.

What Kind of Activities Comprise Advocacy Work?

The list of advocacy-related activities below is not all-inclusive. Each activity includes a recent instance of a specific action taken by active nonprofit organizations around the nation. The list and illustrations can inspire others and offer concepts for future activism on all fronts and in all types of conflicts.

1. **Organizing: Developing power from the bottom up:** The immigrant and refugee populations in Portland, Oregon are organized by the centre for Intercultural Organizing. These gatherings give immigrant leaders a chance to organize their supporters and strengthen their local communities.
2. **Educate legislators: Inform the audience of the issues:** NARAL supports choice Wisconsin provides data sheets on its website for state senators to receive so they are aware of the problems faced by women seeking abortions.
3. **Raising public awareness of the legislative process: Introduce constituents and communities to the legislators who represent them:** The centre for poverty Research and actions organizes an annual citizens day wherein its participants and other Utahns visit the statehouse to speak with their representatives and gain knowledge of the legislative procedure. Legislators are given the tools they need to speak with them face-to-face and discuss the issues that affect their daily lives. Additionally, when communities have a stronger stake in the outcomes of policy debates, they are better able to shape their own future.
4. **Research: Produce relevant resources that reflect the real story of your community:** The "Immigrants and the U.S. Healthcare System" paper was published by the California Immigrant policy centre to debunk stereotype and outline current conditions in the Golden state.
5. **Organizing a rally: Plan a rally by organizing supporters for your cause:** A rally in support of comprehensive immigration reform and an end to immigration raids was held in Washington, D.C. in June 2007 by the Fair Immigration Reform Movement (FIRM), a confederation of pro- immigrant organizations.
6. **Regulatory efforts: At the agencies, take action:** The state Motor Vehicle Administration (MVA) has come under pressure from CASA of Maryland, Inc. to adhere to the law and avoid discriminating against applicants for drivers' licenses based on their capacity to demonstrate legal residency.
7. **Public education:** Inform the public about the problems: Community forums on state and federal immigration issues are occasionally held by rights for all people in Denver, Colorado.

8. **Nonpartisan voter education:** Inform the electorate on the issues: In Los Angeles, California, CARECEN promotes civic engagement among the Latino and immigrant communities and informs the general public on how to take part more actively in elections and civic life.
9. **Encourage voters to caste ballots through nonpartisan voter mobilization:** In the suburban countries around Chicago, the Illinois Coalition for Immigrant and Refugee Rights (ICIRR) launched a massive voter registration and mobilization effort in 2004.
10. **Educational Conferences:** Attend educational conferences to network, share knowledge and make future plans

    The affiliated association of the National Council of La Raza (NCLR) and other organizations meet at an annual conference to discuss problems and solutions that affect the Latino population in the United States.
11. **Training:** The United States Student Association (USSA) sponsors Grassroots Organizing Weekends (GROW) training events that impart effective tactics and abilities for direct action organizing on student-related topics.

Approaches to Policy Advocacy

1. Advising

a. When asking and looking for advice, it is best to go to someone who is an expert in the field - that will look at the situation of policy with objectivity.

b. The experts will talk informally to the key groups or focus groups.

c. Give suggestions and recommendations that they draw from their own experience on how to improve the policies in question.

d. Advisors are the people that will influence the decisions that are made by the decision makers through the recommendations that they make, using their experience.

Media campaigning

a. The message needs to appeal to your audience.

b. Important component of any advocacy campaign is media attention.

c. To ensure that the main points are spoken about, the speaker must be skilled in delivering the 'one minute message'.

d. It means that the person delivering the message is able to provide all of the information that is needed to capture their audience and 'sell' the idea in one minute. The message must start off with a few important words about the current policy and then explain the changes that need to be made in a few words.

e. The words that are used in this message must give the necessary details in the shortest way possible.

2. Lobbying

a. Aim is to persuade or influence the actions of government and to persuade policymakers or private corporations to ensure changes are made to existing policies.
b. Described as speaking directly to the audience, explaining the problems that exist and proposing any solutions to the problems.
c. Important for influencing current policies, laws and programmes. It can be used when your audience is open to listening to your recommendations of potential solutions.

   Examples of lobbying are meetings, policy papers, petitions and briefing papers.

3. Activism

a. Activism is very closely connected to raising awareness and media coverage.
b. The aim of activism is to place public pressure on as many people as possible in order to ensure that there is as much support as possible for their campaign for change to take place.
c. This is done when the audience is swayed by the opinion of the public to make the changes to the policies.
   i. Example of activism is rallies that take place to bring attention to a situation. Another example is signing petitions to fix a problem.

4. Information, Education, Communication (IEC)

a. Done by service providers. Individuals or segments in a community are the target audiences. Main objective is to change behaviour and to raise awareness.
b. Strategies used are mass media campaigns, outreach to communities, sorting the audience and traditional forms of media.
c. The success of IEC is done by making a change to the skills and knowledge of the audience and the community.

5. Behavioural Change Communication (BCC)

a. Interactive process of any intervention, involving individuals, societies or communities and is used to develop communication strategies.
b. The objective is to encourage positive behaviours, build relationships with people that believe in the changes that want encouragement and the organizations and potential communities that will help to make these changes.
c. It is also used when we want to make a long-term campaign sustainable.

Defining Advocacy for Rural Advisory Services (RAS).

a. Advocacy is important in both rural and urban settings and it needs to be done on an ongoing basis for a positive influence on the policy environment.
b. It is crucial that you as an extension actor are as effective as possible.
c. For RAS, advocacy involves promoting, supporting and defending something of great importance – *Ex:* policies that influence rural development.
d. RAS plays an important role as the broker within the Agricultural Innovation System (AIS), providing feedback between the farmers, agri-business, researchers and educators in the system.
e. Supporting people in dealing with any existing difficulties they are facing in order to improve the livelihoods of rural people.
f. RAS and policy advocacy have shown positive effects on the skills and knowledge, adaptation to new technology and productivity of rural communities, even when they are very under-resourced.

Policy Advocacy Strategy

For developing a policy advocacy strategy we followed

1. Identification Of Policy Issues and Solutions

In the policy process, choosing an option for a policy is essentially a choice that is made by the various actors. There is a negotiation that takes place between these actors before making a choice. The choice is made by looking at the research and the data that is collected. This information must be presented in a format that is recognizable to the decision makers. By ensuring that all of the information that is used in the research is understood, the quality and the effectiveness of deciding on policy actions will be improved.

2. Understanding Your Audience

For advocacy, there are various types of audiences, ranging from individuals to entire communities. With regards to advocacy campaigns, there may be more than one specific audience that is applicable. These audiences can include religious and community leaders, concerned parents, or even government and parliamentary leaders. The key objective for making sure that there is effective advocacy is to focus on the audiences that will have the most impact on the decision-making process. In most cases special interest groups should be identified. These are groups within an organization that share your goal and normally include individuals with key skills and connections both at upper organizational levels and within communities.

3. Analyse Channels of Influence

There are two main channels of influence that can be found in the advocacy process. The first channel is described as the primary audience.

a) **The primary audience** are the individuals and groups that are in a position to take the necessary action that is the focus of the advocacy campaign. They are the decision makers that have the main responsibility of planning and managing the programmes. These decisions are the main aim of the advocacy strategy.

Primary Audience

Groups directly involved in the policy making process.

E.g. Government officials, corporations.

The second channel is the secondary audiences. These audiences are those that have the impact to influence the primary audiences. The actions and opinions of the secondary audience are important when it comes to achieving the advocacy objective.

Secondary Audience

Groups able to influence primary audience members through political influence or pressure from public opinion.

E.g. Religious and community leaders.

4. Defining Advocacy Goals and Objectives

Goals with the desired result of any advocacy activity A goal can be described as something that needs to be achieved so that there is progress and you can move forward. Goals for advocacy need to be SMART (Specific, Measurable,

Achievable, Realistic and Time-bound). An advocacy goal is usually seen as a long-term goal and will have a long-term result (3-5 years of advocacy work). The goal is not generally something that you can achieve using your network; it is considered to be external from your network. The important points to note when it comes to goals is that they should be linked to your mission and vision statements, which help you identify the group of people you will need to approach as allies.

SMART Objectives

SMART stands for specific, measurable and monitorable, achievable, realistic and time bound.

A. **Specific:** This means that the advocacy member must use change-focused language rather than activity-focused language. There must be a clear and focused outline of the changes. Make sure that no jargon is used; this could be confusing to those that are not familiar with activity-related wording. Ensure that you are not ambiguous or using phrases that could have a double meaning.

B. **Measurable:** Make sure that the when presenting the evidence, the numbers are manageable; this will make it easier to understand and process. The outcomes need to be measurable. When giving information about the people involved and the length of time it will take, make sure that all that you want to achieve is as exact as possible and ensure that it is credible.

C. **Achievable**: The goals need to be as clear as possible. The goals need to be attainable and they should be practical. They should not be something that just look good theoretically but should be possible to achieve.

D. **Realistic:** The goals need to be a true reflection of what can be achieved. The more realistic the goal, the more credible it is. It is credible because it shows the audience that you have thought it through and you know it is possible.

E. **Time bound:** This means that the goals must be accomplished in a specific amount of time. There needs to be a vibrant timeframe for every goal that you have identified. The timeframe that you have allocated to each goal must be realistic. Generally the timeframe for an advocacy objective is 1-3 years.

5. Developing Advocacy Messages

Advocacy vs BCC and IEC messages

Each of these activities (BCC and IEC) have similarities.

They are all focused specifically on the awareness of specific issues. However, the main focus of BCC and IEC is on changing the behaviour of individuals whereas advocacy is aimed at change on a more collective basis of action and promoting social change.

This change is mostly for community or district levels. Global Forum for Rural Advisory Services BCC and IEC are generally more well-known than advocacy. Throughout training it is very important to highlight the differences to ensure that all of the advocacy objectives and goals are advocacy-related and not BCC- or IEC-related.

6. Select the Message for your Audience

To ensure that your message is taken seriously and it has the right amount of influence, you need to shape the message that you offer to your audience. The message that is described here is the message that you want to get across to the audience. You need to ensure that your message is clear, compelling, accurate and short.

7. Select Advocacy Activities and Communication Tools

Once the audience that you need to target is identified, the next step is for you to decide what the best form of communication to use to deliver your message is. There are various communication tools that you can use, including:

- Lobbying
- Speeches
- Workshops
- Radio
- TV interviews
- Dramas or skits
- Press releases;
- Networking
- Flyers
- Posters
- Video messages

- Social media
- Websites
- Meetings
- Mass actions

1. The face of the Advocacy Campaign/Messenger/Policy Champions

a) **Assess your reputation:** When an advocacy issue is made public, an organization runs the risk of reputation, relationship or partnership damage. A risk investigation will help you to identify the best way to implement the most effective form of advocacy in a business.

b) **Assess your communication and social:** Before you can start with any advocacy, you need to start a network. This must include creating an identity, ensuring that you refine your communication skills through practice and strengthening the decision-making processes and the necessary skills and resources. A communication strategy must have the same amount of principles as any social marketing or advertising campaign.

c) **Identify policy champions:** Identifying policy champions can be a challenging task. Individuals need to be selected based on project needs. The most well-known example of policy champions are celebrity activists. These individuals are able to use their fame to raise money and awareness for important issues but are often not as involved at the policy formation level.

d) **Equipping the policy champions:** In order to give objective feedback to policy champions, there need to be records and evaluations on the behaviour of the champions. There is however, always going to be a degree of subjectivity. In order to evaluate the advocacy effort, it is best to keep the bigger picture regarding your advocacy campaign in mind

3

Policy Analysis

It is a systematic method to solving problems through an examination of policy approaches.

It involves evaluating public policies, including their development, implementation and impacts, to determine their effectiveness in achieving desired outcomes. The process includes identifying relevant issues, assessing potential solutions, weighing the costs and benefits and recommending the most appropriate course of action.

Use of Policy Analysis in Decision-Making

Policy analysis combines qualitative and quantitative methods to assess policies' implications on economic, social and political factors. It often includes stakeholder analysis, forecasting future scenarios and evaluating policy impacts using tools like cost-benefit analysis, risk assessment and statistical modeling

Policy analysis plays a crucial role in decision-making by as long as a structured framework to evaluate the consequences of various policy options. It helps policymakers make informed choices by:

1. **Clarifying objectives and priorities**: Policy analysis identifies the goals and objectives that a policy should achieve, helping decision-makers prioritize actions based on the most pressing needs.
2. **Evaluating alternatives**: It systematically compares different policy options, considering their potential benefits, costs and risks. This comparison enables decision-makers to select the most effective and efficient solution to a particular problem.
3. **Assessing impacts**: Policy analysis provides insights into the potential economic, social and environmental impacts of policies, helping decision-makers understand their broader implications.
4. **Facilitating transparent decision-making**: By employing evidence-based approaches, policy analysis promotes transparency and accountability in decision-making, guaranteeing that decisions are made based on data and scrutiny rather than intuition or political pressure.

5. **Minimizing risks**: It helps identify and mitigate risks linked with diverse policy choices, allowing decision-makers to anticipate potential challenges and develop strategies to address them.

Types of Policy Analysis

Policy analysis can be broadly categorized into different types based on its purpose, methodology and focus. Here is a detailed overview of the main types:

1. Descriptive Policy Analysis

Descriptive policy analysis focuses on understanding and explaining existing policies. It aims to describe the characteristics, processes and outcomes of a policy without necessarily suggesting changes or improvements.

- **Purpose**: To provide a factual account of a policy's design, implementation and effects.
- **Methods**: Uses case studies, historical analysis and qualitative research techniques.
- **Examples**: Analyzing the implementation of a healthcare policy to understand how it was executed and what outcomes were achieved.

2. Normative Policy Analysis

Normative policy analysis evaluates policies based on ethical, moral or value-based criteria. It assesses whether a policy aligns with certain standards, values or principles.

- **Purpose**: To judge the desirability or appropriateness of a policy.
- **Methods**: Uses philosophical reasoning, ethical frameworks and stakeholder perspectives.
- **Examples**: Assessing a social welfare policy based on its fairness and equity.

3. Prescriptive policy analysis

Prescriptive policy analysis focuses on recommending specific courses of action or policy interventions. It is solution-oriented and aims to suggest the best policy option based on evidence and analysis.

- **Purpose**: To provide actionable recommendations to address a policy problem.
- **Methods**: Utilizes cost-benefit analysis, cost-effectiveness analysis and optimization models.

- **Examples**: Recommending policy options to reduce carbon emissions based on a comparative analysis of different strategies.

4. Prospective Policy Analysis

Prospective policy analysis analyses the future impacts of a policy before it is put into effect. It seeks to predict the outcomes, costs and benefits of proposed policies.

- **Purpose**: To forecast the effects of a policy and guide decision-makers in selecting the most effective approach.
- **Methods**: Uses modeling, simulations, scenario analysis and forecasting techniques.
- **Examples**: Analyzing the potential impact of a new tax policy on economic growth and income distribution.

5. Retrospective Policy Analysis

Retrospective policy analysis evaluates the effectiveness of a policy after it has been implemented. It focuses on assessing what worked, what didn't and why.

- **Purpose**: To learn from past policy experiences and improve future policy-making.
- **Methods**: Uses evaluation techniques such as impact assessments, program evaluations and performance reviews.
- **Examples**: Analyzing the outcomes of a public education reform policy five years after its implementation.

6. Process Policy Analysis

Process policy analysis examines the processes involved in policy formulation, development and implementation. It focuses on understanding the steps, stakeholders and contexts that shape policy outcomes.

- **Purpose**: To understand how policies are made and identify potential improvements in the policy-making process.
- **Methods**: Uses case studies, interviews and process mapping techniques.
- **Examples**: Analyzing the stakeholder engagement process in the development of a new transportation policy.

7. Comparative Policy Analysis

Comparative policy analysis involves comparing policies across different contexts, such as countries, regions or sectors. It aims to identify best practices and learn from the experiences of others.

- **Purpose**: To draw lessons from different policy contexts and identify transferable practices.
- **Methods**: Uses comparative case studies, cross-national analysis and benchmarking techniques.
- **Examples**: Comparing healthcare policies in different countries to identify effective approaches to universal health coverage.

8. Cost-Benefit policy analysis

Cost-benefit policy analysis evaluates the financial implications of a policy by comparing its costs against the anticipated benefits. It is often used to determine whether a policy is economically viable or justifiable.

- **Purpose**: To assess the economic efficiency of a policy.
- **Methods**: Utilizes economic models, discounting techniques and valuation methods to estimate costs and benefits.
- **Examples**: Conducting a cost-benefit analysis to decide whether to build a new public infrastructure project.

9. Participatory Policy Analysis

Participatory policy analysis involves engaging stakeholders, including the public, in the policy analysis process. It emphasizes inclusivity, transparency and democratic decision-making.

- **Purpose**: To incorporate diverse perspectives and ensure that policies reflect the needs and preferences of those affected.
- **Methods**: Uses public consultations, surveys, focus groups and participatory workshops.
- **Examples**: Developing a community-based environmental policy through participatory methods involving local residents.

Process of Analysis

The process of policy analysis involves several systematic steps to evaluate and improve public policies. This structured approach ensures that policies are effective, efficient and aligned with the desired outcomes. Below is a full description of the policy analysis process:

1. Problem Definition

The first step in policy analysis is defining the problem that the policy aims to address. This involves understanding the nature, scope and causes of the issue. Analysts gather data, identify the stakeholders affected and clarify the problem's dimensions to frame it accurately. A well-defined problem provides a clear focus for subsequent analysis.

- **Purpose**: To ensure a precise understanding of the issue at hand.
- **Activities**: Conducting literature reviews, consulting stakeholders and using data analysis to identify key aspects of the problem.

2. Establishing Evaluation Criteria

Once the problem is defined, the next step is to establish criteria to evaluate potential policy options. These criteria could include effectiveness, efficiency, equity, feasibility and political acceptability. The evaluation criteria help in systematically comparing different policy alternatives to determine which best meets the objectives.

- **Purpose**: To create a basis for comparing policy options.
- **Activities**: Defining measurable indicators, consulting with stakeholders and aligning criteria with policy goals.

3. Identifying Policy Alternatives

After establishing evaluation criteria, policy analysts identify and develop various alternatives or options to address the problem. This step involves brainstorming possible solutions, reviewing existing policies and considering innovative approaches. It also includes narrowing down options to a manageable number that can be analyzed in depth.

- **Purpose**: To generate a comprehensive list of feasible policy options.
- **Activities**: Literature reviews, expert consultations and brainstorming sessions.

4. Assessing Policy Alternatives

In this step, each policy alternative is evaluated against the criteria established earlier. Analysts examine the potential costs, benefits, risks and impacts of each option. They use tools like cost-benefit analysis, cost-effectiveness analysis and multi-criteria decision analysis to assess how well each policy meets the desired objectives.

- **Purpose**: To determine the relative merits and drawbacks of each policy option.
- **Activities**: Quantitative analysis (*e.g.*, cost-benefit analysis) and qualitative assessments (*e.g.*, stakeholder opinions, ethical considerations).

5. Recommending the Best Policy Option

Based on the assessment, analysts recommend the most suitable policy option or a combination of options. This recommendation is supported by evidence gathered during the analysis, including data, projections and stakeholder inputs. The recommendation must consider not only the best solution but also its feasibility, acceptability and sustainability.

- **Purpose**: To provide decision-makers with clear, evidence-based advice on the most effective policy option.
- **Activities**: Writing policy briefs, creating reports and presenting findings to decision-makers.

6. Communicating Findings

Effective communication is crucial in policy analysis. Analysts must present their findings and recommendations to policymakers, stakeholders and the public in a clear, concise and persuasive manner. This may involve preparing reports, executive summaries, presentations or public briefings.

- **Purpose**: To ensure that decision-makers understand the analysis and its implications.
- **Activities**: Drafting policy documents, creating visual aids and holding meetings or briefings.

7. Monitoring and Evaluating the Implemented Policy

The final step is to monitor and evaluate the implemented policy to assess its performance over time. This involves tracking key indicators, collecting data and comparing outcomes against the policy's goals and evaluation criteria. Continuous monitoring helps identify any unintended consequences or areas for improvement.

- **Purpose**: To ensure that the policy achieves its objectives and to inform future policy decisions.
- **Activities**: Conducting evaluations, collecting feedback and making adjustments as needed

Methods and Techniques Commonly Used in Policy Analysis

Policy analysis uses various methods and techniques to systematically evaluate policy options, predict outcomes and make recommendations. Each method or technique is designed to address specific aspects of policy-making, such as assessing costs and benefits, understanding stakeholder perspectives or predicting future scenarios. Here is a detailed description of different methods and techniques commonly used in policy analysis:

1. Cost-Benefit Analysis (CBA)

Cost-benefit analysis is a quantitative method used to evaluate the economic efficiency of a policy by comparing its costs with its anticipated benefits. It assigns a monetary value to all costs and benefits, allowing for a straightforward comparison.

- **Purpose**: To determine whether the benefits of a policy outweigh its costs and to identify the option that provides the greatest net benefit.
- **Techniques**: Estimating direct and indirect costs, discounting future costs and benefits to present value and calculating the net present value (NPV) or benefit-cost ratio (BCR).
- **Applications**: Commonly used in infrastructure projects, environmental regulation and health interventions to assess economic viability.

2. Cost-Effectiveness Analysis (CEA)

Cost-effectiveness analysis is similar to cost-benefit analysis but focuses on comparing the relative costs of achieving a specific outcome or objective, without assigning a monetary value to the benefits.

- **Purpose**: To identify the least costly way to achieve a specific policy goal.
- **Techniques**: Calculating cost-effectiveness ratios, comparing the costs per unit of outcome (*e.g.*, cost per life saved or cost per ton of pollution reduced).
- **Applications**: Frequently used in healthcare and social programs to determine the most efficient allocation of resources for achieving desired outcomes.

3. Multi-Criteria Decision Analysis (MCDA)

Multi-criteria decision analysis is a method used to evaluate policy options based on multiple criteria, including economic, social, environmental and political factors. It allows for the inclusion of both quantitative and qualitative criteria.

- **Purpose**: To make comprehensive decisions by considering various factors that are important to stakeholders.
- **Techniques**: Developing a criteria weighting system, scoring policy alternatives against each criterion and aggregating scores to determine the best option.

- **Applications**: Used in complex decision-making scenarios where multiple, often conflicting, objectives need to be balanced (*e.g.*, urban planning, energy policy).

4. Scenario Analysis

Scenario analysis involves developing different possible future scenarios to assess how various policy options might perform under different conditions. This method is particularly useful for dealing with uncertainty and complexity.

- **Purpose**: To understand the potential impacts of different policies under various future scenarios.
- **Techniques**: Creating narratives or models for different future states, assessing policy outcomes for each scenario and identifying robust policy options.
- **Applications**: Commonly used in environmental policy, disaster preparedness and long-term strategic planning.

5. Regression Analysis

Regression analysis is a statistical technique used to identify and quantify the relationships between variables. It assists in understanding how different elements influence a specific outcome.

- **Purpose**: To predict policy outcomes based on historical data and identify causal relationships.
- **Techniques**: Using linear or multiple regression models to estimate the impact of one or more independent variables on a dependent variable.
- **Applications**: Frequently used in economic policy, social sciences and health studies to evaluate the impact of policies on specific outcomes.

6. Delphi Method

The Delphi method is a qualitative technique that uses iterative rounds of surveys to gather expert opinions and reach a consensus on complex policy issues.

- **Purpose**: To harness expert knowledge and build consensus on policy options.
- **Techniques**: Conducting multiple rounds of anonymous surveys, summarizing feedback and refining questions to achieve convergence of opinions.
- **Applications**: Used in forecasting, strategic planning and situations where expert judgment is crucial (*e.g.*, public health emergencies, defense policy).

7. Stakeholder Analysis

Stakeholder analysis identifies and evaluates the interests, influence and perspectives of all parties affected by or involved in a policy decision. This method helps ensure that policy development is inclusive and considers diverse viewpoints.

- **Purpose:** To understand the positions, interests and power dynamics of different stakeholders.
- **Techniques:** Mapping stakeholders, conducting interviews or surveys and assessing stakeholder influence and interest in the policy issue.
- **Applications:** Used in public policy development, community engagement and conflict resolution to ensure that policies are socially acceptable and politically feasible.

8. Policy Mapping

Policy mapping is a visual method that outlines the relationships, processes and flow of decision-making in a policy area. It helps to understand the policy environment, identify key actors and map out the sequence of decisions.

- **Purpose**: To provide a visual representation of the policy landscape and clarify the policy-making process.
- **Techniques**: Creating flowcharts, diagrams and process maps to represent policy components, interactions and decision points.
- **Applications**: Used to analyze the policy environment in complex sectors like healthcare, education and transportation.

9. Program Evaluation

Program evaluation is a method used to assess the effectiveness, efficiency and impact of a policy or program after it has been implemented. It uses both qualitative and quantitative techniques to determine whether the program meets its intended objectives.

- **Purpose**: To assess the performance of a policy and make adjustments as needed.
- **Techniques**: Using outcome evaluations, process evaluations and impact assessments to determine the program's effectiveness.
- **Applications**: Commonly used in social programs, public health and education to evaluate program outcomes and improve future policy development.

10. Ethnographic Methods

Ethnographic methods involve in-depth, qualitative research techniques such as participant observation, interviews and case studies to understand the cultural, social and political contexts in which policies operate.

- **Purpose**: To gain deep insights into how policies affect people's lives and social dynamics.
- **Techniques**: Conducting fieldwork, engaging with communities and analyzing qualitative data to capture the lived experiences of stakeholders.
- **Applications**: Used in social policy, public health and community development to understand the ground-level impact of policies.

Ethical Policy Analysis

It focuses on evaluating public policies through the lens of moral and ethical principles. It considers not just the efficiency or effectiveness of a policy but also whether it aligns with values such as justice, fairness, equity and human rights. The following are various methods and techniques used specifically for conducting ethical policy analysis:

1. Normative Ethical Frameworks

Normative ethical frameworks provide a structured approach to evaluate policies based on fundamental ethical principles. Analysts use these frameworks to assess whether a policy is morally justifiable or aligns with certain ethical theories.

- **Purpose**: To evaluate policies against established ethical principles such as utilitarianism, deontology, virtue ethics or care ethics.
- **Techniques**:
  - **Utilitarian analysis**: Assesses whether a policy maximizes overall happiness or welfare (greatest good for the greatest number). This involves weighing the benefits and harms to all stakeholders.
  - **Deontological analysis**: Examines whether a policy respects certain moral rules or duties (*e.g.*, rights to freedom, privacy or autonomy). Policies are judged based on adherence to ethical norms, regardless of the outcomes.
  - **Virtue ethics analysis**: Focuses on the character and intentions behind a policy decision, assessing whether it reflects virtues like honesty, compassion or justice.

    - **Care ethics analysis**: Emphasizes relationships and the duty to care for others, particularly vulnerable or marginalized groups.
- **Applications**: Commonly used in healthcare, human rights policies and social justice issues where ethical considerations are paramount.

2. Rights-based Analysis

Rights-based analysis evaluates policies based on their impact on individual and collective rights. It focuses on ensuring that policies respect and protect human rights as enshrined in laws, constitutions or international agreements.

- **Purpose**: To ensure that policies do not infringe upon fundamental human rights.
- **Techniques**:
    - **Legal and ethical audits**: Reviewing policies to determine if they comply with national and international human rights standards.
    - **Stakeholder impact assessment**: Identifying and assessing how policies affect the rights of different stakeholder groups, particularly marginalized populations.
    - **Scoring and ranking**: Using a scoring system to rank policy options based on their alignment with human rights principles.
- **Applications**: Used in areas like criminal justice reform, refugee policies and social welfare programs to evaluate their conformity with human rights obligations.

3. Equity and Social Justice Analysis

Equity and social justice analysis focuses on whether a policy promotes fairness and equality. It examines the distributional impacts of a policy to ensure that it does not disproportionately benefit or harm certain groups.

- **Purpose**: To assess how policies affect different social groups and promote social justice.
- **Techniques**:
    - **Distributional impact analysis**: Analyzes how the benefits and costs of a policy are distributed across different population groups (*e.g.*, by income, race, gender or age).
    - **Intersectional analysis**: Examines how multiple forms of discrimination (*e.g.*, race, gender, disability) intersect to affect groups differently, ensuring that policies do not exacerbate existing inequalities.

    - **Justice mapping**: Visual tools like maps or charts are used to show how resources, services or benefits are distributed and highlight areas of inequity.
- **Applications**: Applied in urban planning, healthcare, education and social welfare policies to ensure equitable outcomes.

4. Participatory Ethical Analysis

Participatory ethical analysis involves engaging stakeholders, including marginalized and affected communities, in the policy analysis process to understand their values, preferences and ethical concerns.

- **Purpose**: To democratize the policy-making process and incorporate diverse ethical perspectives.
- **Techniques**:
    - **Deliberative democracy techniques**: Methods like public forums, focus groups, citizen juries or participatory workshops to gather input from diverse stakeholders.
    - **Surveys and interviews**: Collecting qualitative data on stakeholder values, concerns and ethical preferences.
    - **Consensus building**: Facilitating discussions among stakeholders to reach a shared understanding or agreement on ethical policy issues.
- **Applications**: Used in community development, environmental policy, public health and social services to ensure policies reflect community values and are socially acceptable.

5. Ethical Risk Assessment

Ethical risk assessment evaluates the potential ethical risks or unintended consequences of a policy, including harm to vulnerable populations, violations of rights or exacerbation of inequalities.

- **Purpose**: To identify and mitigate potential ethical risks associated with a policy.
- **Techniques**:
    - **Scenario analysis**: Developing different scenarios to explore potential ethical risks or negative outcomes associated with policy options.
    - **Ethical Impact Assessment (EIA)**: A structured process to assess the ethical implications of a policy, including potential harms and benefits to different groups.

    - **Sensitivity analysis**: Testing how changes in key assumptions or inputs affect the ethical outcomes of a policy, identifying factors that could lead to unethical consequences.
- **Applications**: Applied in public health (*e.g.*, pandemic response), technology policies (*e.g.*, AI ethics) and environmental regulation (*e.g.*, climate justice).

6. Value-Focused Thinking (VFT)

Value-focused thinking is a method that emphasizes identifying and prioritizing values that are important to stakeholders before generating policy alternatives. Instead of focusing solely on solving problems, VFT starts by clarifying values to guide policy decisions.

- **Purpose**: To ensure that policy decisions are aligned with core values and ethical principles.
- **Techniques**
    - **Values hierarchy**: Creating a hierarchy of values (*e.g.*, safety, equity, autonomy) to identify which are most important in the context of a policy decision.
    - **Value clarification workshops**: Engaging stakeholders in discussions to articulate their values and how they relate to policy choices.
    - **Decision trees**: Using decision trees to map out policy options and their alignment with prioritized values.

Tools for Policy Impact Research

Tools for policy impact research are essential in evaluating how policies affect their target populations, sectors or environments. These tools help researchers gather, analyze and interpret data to assess the real-world effects of policies, thereby aiding in evidence-based decision-making and policy refinement.

1. Quantitative Research Tools

Quantitative tools use numerical data and statistical methods to measure policy impact. They provide objective, measurable evidence on the extent and nature of policy outcomes.

- **Purpose**: To objectively measure the effects of policies using statistical data.
- **Techniques**
    - **Surveys and questionnaires**: Tools used to collect large amounts of data from a sample population. Surveys can be designed to measure specific outcomes or changes resulting from a policy.

Application: Used to assess public opinion, behavior changes or service satisfaction following policy implementation.

- **Administrative data analysis**: Utilizes existing data collected by government agencies or organizations (*e.g.*, health records, school attendance rates, employment data) to evaluate policy impact.

  Application: Commonly used in social welfare, public health and education policy analysis.

- **Regression analysis**: A statistical method used to determine the relationship between policy interventions (independent variables) and outcomes (dependent variables).

  Application: Used to control for confounding variables and isolate the effect of a specific policy.

- **Randomized Controlled Trials (RCTs)**: Experiments where participants are randomly assigned to either the intervention group (policy) or control group (no policy) to determine the causal effects of a policy.

Application: Used in fields like healthcare, social programs and education to test the efficacy of new policies or interventions.

2. Qualitative Research Tools

Qualitative tools provide in-depth insights into the social, cultural and contextual factors influencing policy impact. These tools are essential for understanding the lived experiences and perceptions of stakeholders affected by policies.

- **Purpose**: To gain a deeper understanding of the subjective and contextual factors related to policy impact.
- **Techniques**:
  - **Interviews**: Structured, semi-structured or unstructured conversations with key stakeholders to gather detailed information about their experiences, perceptions and attitudes toward a policy.

    Application: Used to explore complex issues like stakeholder attitudes, policy acceptance and barriers to implementation.

  - **Focus groups**: Group discussions facilitated to gather diverse perspectives on a policy issue. Focus groups provide insights into how different groups perceive and experience a policy.

    Application: Often used to understand community responses, stakeholder concerns or cultural implications of policies.

- **Case studies**: In-depth, contextual analyses of specific instances where a policy was implemented. Case studies explore the "how" and "why" of policy impacts in particular settings.

  Application: Used to explore unique or complex policy contexts, such as local governance or community-based interventions.

- **Ethnography:** Involves the detailed study of people and their cultures, observing how policies affect them in their natural environments.

  Application: Used in social policy research, such as community development or health policy, to understand the real-life context of policy impacts.

3. Mixed Methods Research Tools

Mixed methods combine both quantitative and qualitative research techniques to provide a comprehensive analysis of policy impact. This approach collects both numerical data and context-related data.

- **Purpose**: To leverage the strengths of both quantitative and qualitative data for a more holistic understanding of policy impact.
- **Techniques**
  - **Sequential explanatory design**: Involves collecting and analyzing quantitative data first, followed by qualitative data to explain or elaborate on the quantitative findings.

    Application: Used to assess the impact of a policy through statistical data and then explain the reasons behind the trends using qualitative insights.

  - **Concurrent triangulation design**: Simultaneously collects both quantitative and qualitative data to cross-validate and corroborate findings.

    Application: Used in health policy research where quantitative data from health records is corroborated with qualitative data from patient interviews.

  - **Embedded design**: A primary method (qualitative or quantitative) is supplemented by a secondary method to enhance the overall analysis.

    Application: Used in complex policy evaluations where one type of data is insufficient to address all research questions.

4. Geospatial Analysis Tools

Geospatial analysis tools use Geographic Information Systems (GIS) and spatial data to analyze the spatial dimensions of policy impact. They help in visualizing data geographically and understanding the geographic patterns and correlations of policy effects.

- **Purpose**: To analyze spatial data and visualize the geographic distribution of policy impacts.
- **Techniques**:
  - **Geographic Information Systems (GIS)**: Software that captures, stores, analyzes and visualizes spatial data. GIS is used to map policy impact areas, identify hotspots and analyze spatial trends.

    Application: Used in urban planning, environmental policy and public health to visualize the distribution of resources or incidents.
  - **Remote sensing**: Uses satellite imagery and aerial photography to collect data on environmental changes, land use or other spatial phenomena relevant to policy analysis.

    Application: Used in environmental policy to monitor deforestation, urban sprawl or climate change impacts.
  - **Spatial econometrics**: Combines econometric techniques with spatial data to analyze spatial relationships and dependencies in policy impacts.

    Application: Used in regional economic policy, transportation and public health to study spatial interactions and diffusion effects.

5. Modeling and Simulation Tools

Modeling and simulation tools use mathematical, computational or statistical models to simulate the potential outcomes of different policy scenarios. They help policymakers understand the potential consequences of decisions under varying conditions.

- **Purpose**: To predict policy outcomes, explore different scenarios and assess potential impacts.
- **Techniques**:
  - **System dynamics modeling**: A method used to understand the behavior of complex systems over time, using stocks, flows, feedback loops and time delays.

    Application: Used in health policy, environmental policy and economic forecasting to simulate long-term impacts.
  - **Agent-Based Modeling (ABM)**: Simulates interactions among individual agents (*e.g.*, people organizations) to assess how these interactions produce emergent phenomena.

Application: Used in social policy, urban planning and public health to model individual behavior and its effects on policy outcomes.

- **Micro-simulation models**: Uses detailed individual-level data to simulate the impact of policy changes on a micro-level (*e.g.*, households, businesses).

  Application: Often used in tax policy, social security and labor market analysis to predict the distributional effects of policy changes.

6. Participatory Research Tools

Participatory research tools involve engaging stakeholders, including the communities affected by a policy, in the research process. These tools ensure that the perspectives and experiences of all relevant groups are considered.

- **Purpose**: To include diverse stakeholder perspectives in the policy impact analysis.
- **Techniques**:
  - **Participatory Rural Appraisal (PRA)**: A set of participatory tools and methods used to enable rural communities to share, enhance and analyze their knowledge of life and conditions to plan and act.

    Application: Used in rural development, agricultural policy and community health to incorporate local knowledge and preferences.
  - **Community-Based Participatory Research (CBPR)**: Involves researchers and community members as equal partners in the research process, from designing the study to analyzing data and disseminating results.

    Application: Used in public health, environmental justice and urban development to ensure research reflects community needs and priorities.
  - **Deliberative polling**: Combines opinion polling with deliberative democracy methods to gauge informed public opinion on policy issues.

    Application: Used in democratic governance and policy deliberation to understand well-considered public preferences.

Context Assessment Tools

Context assessment tools are essential in policy impact research as they help evaluate the environment and conditions surrounding a policy. Understanding the context in which a policy is implemented is crucial for assessing its effectiveness and identifying factors that might influence its success or failure.

These tools help researchers and policymakers gather relevant background information, analyze existing conditions and identify the key variables affecting policy outcomes.

1. Situational analysis

Situational analysis involves examining the current conditions and factors that might affect the implementation and outcomes of a policy. It provides a comprehensive overview of the environment in which the policy operates.

- **Purpose**: To understand the existing situation, including social, economic, political and environmental factors that may impact policy implementation.
- **Techniques**
  - **SWOT analysis (Strengths, Weaknesses, Opportunities, Threats)**: A strategic planning tool used to identify internal strengths and weaknesses of a policy initiative, as well as external opportunities and threats.

    Application: Helps in understanding the internal capabilities and external factors that could influence policy effectiveness.
  - **PEST analysis (Political, Economic, Social, Technological)**: Examines the external macro-environmental factors that could impact policy outcomes.

    Application: Useful for assessing how political, economic, social and technological changes might affect the policy environment.
  - **Contextual analysis**: Focuses on specific contextual factors such as cultural norms, institutional settings and historical factors.

    Application: Provides insights into how local contexts might influence policy implementation and acceptance.

2. Stakeholder Analysis

Stakeholder analysis identifies and assesses the interests, influence and relationships of different stakeholders involved in or affected by a policy. Understanding stakeholders is crucial for designing and implementing effective policies.

- **Purpose**: To map out the key stakeholders, their interests and their potential influence on the policy process.
- **Techniques**:
  - **Stakeholder mapping**: Visual representation of stakeholders based on their level of influence and interest in the policy.

Application: Helps in prioritizing stakeholder engagement and understanding their potential impact on policy outcomes.

- **Power-interest grid**: Categorizes stakeholders based on their power and interest levels, helping to tailor communication and engagement strategies.

  Application: Useful for managing stakeholder relationships and addressing their concerns appropriately.

- **Influence-impact matrix**: Analyzes the degree to which stakeholders can influence policy outcomes and the extent of the policy's impact on them.

  Application: Assists in identifying key players who need to be actively involved in the policy process.

3. Mixed Methods Research Tools

4. Geospatial Analysis tools

5. Modeling and Simulation Tools

6. Participatory Research Tools

Communication tools

Communication tools for policy impact are crucial for effectively disseminating information about policies, engaging stakeholders and ensuring that policy-related messages are clear and impactful. These tools help bridge the gap between policymakers and the public, enhance transparency and facilitate dialogue about policy issues. Here's a detailed description of various communication tools used in policy impact research:

1. Policy Briefs

Policy briefs are concise documents that summarize key findings, recommendations and implications of research or policy analysis. They are designed to inform policymakers and stakeholders quickly and clearly.

- **Purpose**: To provide a succinct overview of policy issues, research findings and recommendations.
- **Features**:
  - **Summary of findings**: Presents the key results of the research or analysis.
  - **Policy recommendations**: Provides actionable suggestions based on the findings.

- **Background information**: Offers context and background relevant to the issue.
- **Application**: Used to inform decision-makers and stakeholders about important issues and evidence in a brief and accessible format.

2. Info-graphics

Info-graphics are graphical representations of information, data, or knowledge meant to convey complicated information quickly and clearly. They combine graphics, charts and text to communicate key messages.

- **Purpose**: To visually convey information and make data more accessible and engaging.
- **Features**
  - **Visual elements**: Uses graphs, charts, icons and images to illustrate data and concepts.
  - **Concise text**: Provides brief and focused explanations to accompany visual elements.
  - **Design principles**: Utilizes design elements such as color, layout and typography to enhance readability and impact.
- **Application**: Effective for communicating data-driven findings and making complex information more understandable to a broader audience.

3. Needs Assessment

Needs assessment determines the needs and priorities of the target population that the policy aims to address. It helps in identifying gaps between current conditions and desired outcomes.

- **Purpose**: To identify and prioritize the needs of the population that the policy is intended to serve.
- **Techniques**
  - **Community needs assessment**: Involves collecting data from community members through surveys, interviews and focus groups to identify their needs and preferences.

    Application: Helps in tailoring policies to better meet the needs of specific communities or populations.
  - **Gap analysis**: Compares current conditions with desired conditions to identify gaps and areas for improvement.

    Application: Useful for pinpointing specific issues that the policy needs to address.

- **Participatory needs assessment**: Engages stakeholders and community members in identifying and prioritizing their needs, ensuring that their voices are heard.

  Application: Ensures that the needs assessment process is inclusive and reflects the perspectives of those affected by the policy.

4. Policy Environment Analysis

Policy environment analysis examines the broader environment in which a policy is formulated and implemented, including legal, institutional and economic factors.

- **Purpose**: To understand the external factors that could affect the policy process and its outcomes.
- **Techniques**
  - **Institutional analysis**: Evaluates the role and capacity of institutions involved in policy implementation, including their structure, functions and resources.

    Application: Helps in understanding how institutional factors might impact policy effectiveness.
  - **Legal and regulatory analysis**: Assesses the legal and regulatory framework governing the policy area to identify potential constraints or opportunities.

    Application: Useful for identifying legal barriers or supportive regulations that could affect policy implementation.
  - **Economic analysis**: Examines the economic conditions and factors that could influence the policy, such as funding, economic incentives and cost-benefit considerations.

    Application: Helps in assessing the economic feasibility and impact of the policy.

5. Historical Analysis

Historical analysis involves studying the historical context and past experiences related to similar policies or issues. It provides insights into how past policies were implemented and their outcomes.

- **Purpose**: To learn from past experiences and historical trends that may influence current policy decisions.
- **Techniques**:
  - **Historical case studies**: Analyzes previous policy interventions or historical events to draw lessons and identify patterns.

Application: Useful for understanding how similar policies have been implemented in the past and their outcomes.

- **Trend analysis**: Examines historical data and trends to predict future developments and inform policy decisions.

  Application: Helps in anticipating future challenges and opportunities based on historical patterns.

These context assessment tools help researchers and policymakers gather a comprehensive understanding of the environment in which a policy is implemented. By analyzing the situational, stakeholder, needs, policy environment and historical contexts, these tools ensure that policies are designed and implemented with a thorough understanding of their surroundings and potential impacts

Policy Influence Tools

Policy influence tools are strategies and methods used to shape, guide or sway policy decisions and outcomes. These tools help stakeholders, advocates and researchers effectively influence the policymaking process to achieve desired outcomes. Here is a comprehensive overview of various policy influence tools, including their purposes, techniques and references:

1. Advocacy Campaigns

Advocacy campaigns involve organized efforts to influence public opinion and policymakers to support specific policy changes or initiatives.

- **Purpose**: To mobilize public support, raise awareness and persuade policymakers to adopt or modify policies.
- **Techniques**
  - **Public awareness campaigns**: Use media, advertisements and public events to inform the public and garner support for a cause.

    Application: Effective in drawing attention to issues and generating public pressure on policymakers.

  - **Lobbying**: Direct interaction with policymakers to advocate for specific policy positions or changes.

    Application: Involves meetings, briefings and presentations to persuade decision-makers.

  - **Grassroots mobilization**: Engages the public in advocacy efforts, often through community organizing, petitions and social media.

    Application: Builds a broad base of support and puts pressure on policymakers from multiple fronts.

2. Policy Networks and Coalitions

Policy networks and coalitions involve groups of organizations or individuals working together to influence policy outcomes by pooling resources, expertise and advocacy efforts.

- **Purpose**: To amplify influence through collaboration and collective action.
- **Techniques**:
  - **Forming coalitions**: Building alliances among stakeholders with shared interests to strengthen advocacy efforts.

    Application: Enhances the credibility and reach of policy proposals by uniting diverse voices.
  - **Networking**: Establishing connections with influential policymakers, experts and other stakeholders.

    Application: Facilitates information exchange, collaboration and influence over policy discussions.
  - **Strategic partnerships**: Partnering with organizations that have complementary goals or resources to enhance advocacy efforts.

    Application: Leveraging joint resources and expertise to increase impact.

3. Policy Analysis and Evidence-based Research

Policy analysis and evidence-based research involve generating and presenting data, analysis and evidence to support policy recommendations and influence decision-making.

- **Purpose**: To provide policymakers with rigorous, evidence-based information to guide policy choices.
- **Techniques**:
  - **Cost-Benefit Analysis (CBA)**: Evaluates the economic advantages and disadvantages of policy options to inform decision-making.

    Application: Helps policymakers understand the financial implications and trade-offs of different policy alternatives.
  - **Impact assessments**: Assesses the potential effects of proposed policies on various outcomes such as social, economic and environmental factors.

    Application: Provides a comprehensive view of the potential impacts of policy decisions.

- **Systematic reviews**: Synthesizes existing research and evidence on a particular issue to offer a consolidated view of what is known.

  Application: Supports evidence-based policymaking by summarizing the current state of knowledge.

4. Strategic Ccommunication

Strategic communication involves developing and implementing communication strategies designed to influence public opinion and policy outcomes.

- **Purpose**: To effectively convey messages, shape perceptions and build support for policy initiatives.
- **Techniques**
  - **Message framing**: Crafting messages that highlight specific aspects of an issue to influence how it is perceived.

    Application: Shapes public and policymaker perceptions by emphasizing certain elements of a policy.
  - **Media relations**: Engaging with media outlets to secure coverage and shape the narrative around policy issues.

    Application: Ensures that key messages reach a wide audience and are presented in a favorable light.
  - **Public engagement**: Organizing events, town halls and forums to discuss policy issues and gather feedback.

    Application: Enhances transparency and builds support by involving the public in policy discussions.

5. Public Participation and Deliberative Processes

Public participation and deliberative processes involve engaging the public and stakeholders in discussions and decision-making about policy issues.

- **Purpose**: To ensure that policy decisions reflect the preferences and needs of the affected communities.
- **Techniques**:
  - **Deliberative democracy**: Involves structured deliberation where participants discuss and debate policy issues to reach consensus or informed opinions.

    Application: Provides a platform for diverse voices and perspectives to shape policy outcomes.

- **Citizen panels**: Groups of citizens are recruited to provide input on policy issues and participate in decision-making processes.

  Application: Engages the public in policy development and ensures that decisions are grounded in public opinion.

- **Participatory budgeting**: Allows community members to have a direct role in deciding how public funds are allocated.

  Application: Empowers citizens and enhances accountability by involving them in budgetary decisions.

6. Political Advocacy and Lobbying

Political advocacy and lobbying involve direct efforts to influence policymakers and political processes through persuasion, negotiation and advocacy.

- **Purpose**: To shape legislative and regulatory decisions by directly engaging with policymakers and political actors.
- **Techniques**:
  - **Lobbying**: Engaging directly with legislators and government officials to advocate for specific policy positions.

    Application: Influences the legislative process and policy outcomes through targeted advocacy.

  - **Political Action Committees (PACs)**: Organizations that raise and spend money to influence elections and policy decisions.

    Application: Supports candidates and policies that align with the organization's goals.

  - **Grassroots advocacy**: Mobilizing citizens to advocate for policy changes through petitions, rallies and direct communication with policymakers.

    Application: Builds broad-based support and puts pressure on policymakers from the ground up.

These policy influence tools enable stakeholders, advocates and researchers to effectively shape policy decisions and outcomes. By utilizing a combination of advocacy campaigns, policy networks, evidence-based research, strategic communication, public participation and political lobbying, these tools help in driving policy changes and ensuring that decisions are informed and effective

4

Policy Development Process

The policy development process is a structured approach to creating policies that address specific issues or achieve particular goals. It involves several steps, from identifying the problem to implementing and evaluating the policy

Steps of Policy Development Process

1. Problem identification

- **Definition**: The process of recognizing and defining an issue that requires government intervention.
- **Key actors**
  - **Public**: Citizens, interest groups and communities often raise awareness about problems.
  - **Media**: Plays a critical role in highlighting issues and shaping public opinion.
  - **Policymakers**: Government officials, legislators and public administrators who prioritize issues.
  - **Experts and academics**: Provide data, research and analysis that help frame problems.

2. Policy Formulation

- **Definition**: The development of possible solutions to the identified problem.
- **Key Actors**:
  - **Legislators**: Draft and propose policies.
  - **Government Agencies**: Provide technical expertise and help design feasible policies.
  - **Think Tanks and research institutions**: Offer policy recommendations based on evidence and research.
  - **Interest Groups**: Lobby for specific policy solutions that align with their interests.

3. Policy Adoption

- **Definition**: The formal decision-making process where a policy is accepted and authorized by the relevant governing bodies.
- **Key actors**:
  - **Legislatures**: Debate, amend and vote on proposed policies.
  - **Executive branch**: Presidents, governors or mayors who sign policies into law.
  - **Judiciary**: May be involved if there are legal challenges to the policy.
  - **Political parties**: Influence policy adoption through their platforms and the positions of their members.

4. Policy Implementation

- **Definition**: The process of putting adopted policies into action.
- **Key actors**:
  - **Government agencies**: Execute and enforce the policy.
  - **Local governments**: Often responsible for the on-the-ground implementation.
  - **Non-Governmental Organizations (NGOs)**: May assist in implementation, especially in areas like public health or education.
  - **Private sector**: Can be involved in implementation through public-private partnerships.

5. Policy Evaluation

- **Definition**: Assessing the effectiveness of a policy after its implementation.
- **Key actors**:
  - **Evaluation agencies**: Specialized government or independent bodies that measure policy outcomes.
  - **Academics and researchers**: Conduct studies and evaluations to assess policy impact.
  - **Public feedback**: Citizens and stakeholders provide input on the policy's success or shortcomings.

Environmental Factors

- **Political environment**: The ideological and political landscape, including the distribution of power among parties and the influence of lobbyists.

- **Economic environment**: Budgetary constraints, economic conditions and resources available for policy implementation.
- **Social environment**: Public opinion, social movements and demographic trends that affect policy priorities.
- **Technological environment**: Advances in technology that can influence both the problems identified and the solutions proposed.
- **Legal environment**: The existing laws, regulations and legal precedents that shape policy options.

Stakeholder Mapping, Identifying Opportunities and Barriers

Stakeholder mapping is a strategic tool used to identify, analyze and visualize the key stakeholders involved in or affected by a policy, project or decision. It helps in understanding the influence and interest of different stakeholders, which is crucial for effective decision-making and communication strategies. Here's how to approach stakeholder mapping:

Steps in Stakeholder Mapping

1. Identify Stakeholders

Individuals, group organizations or institutions that have an interest in or are affected by the policy or project.

Types of Stakeholders

- **Primary stakeholders**: Directly affected by the outcome (*e.g.*, citizens, employees, customers).
- **Secondary stakeholders**: Indirectly affected or involved (*e.g.*, suppliers, local communities, NGOs).
- **Key stakeholders**: Those with significant influence or power over the policy (*e.g.*, government officials, investors, industry leaders)

2. Analyze Stakeholders

- **Assess interests**: What are the needs, concerns and objectives of each stakeholder?
- **Determine influence**: How much power or influence does each stakeholder have over the policy or project?
- **Understand relationships**: How do stakeholders relate to each other? Are there alliances or conflicts?

3. Prioritize Stakeholders

Map influence and interest: Use a stakeholder matrix to categorize stakeholders based on their level of interest and influence:

a) **High influence, high interest**: Engage closely and actively manage their expectations.
b) **High influence, low interest**: Keep satisfied; involve them as needed.
c) **Low influence, high interest**: Keep informed and ensure their concerns are considered.
d) **Low influence, low interest**: Monitor with minimal effort.

4. Develop Engagement Strategies

- **Tailor communication**: Develop specific communication strategies for each stakeholder group based on their interest and influence.
- **Involve stakeholders**: Engage key stakeholders in decision-making processes to ensure their support.
- **Address concerns**: Proactively address any concerns or opposition from stakeholders to minimize resistance.

5. Monitor and Adjust

- **Regular review**: Continuously monitor stakeholder positions, influence and relationships as they can change over time.
- **Adapt strategies**: Adjust engagement strategies as needed to maintain support and manage opposition.

Stakeholder Mapping Tools

- **Stakeholder matrix**: A 2x2 grid that plots stakeholders based on their level of influence and interest.
- **Power/interest grid**: A visual tool similar to the stakeholder matrix but often used in project management contexts.
- **Stakeholder influence diagrams**: Visual maps showing the influence pathways between stakeholders.
- **Venn diagrams**: Useful for showing overlapping interests among stakeholders.

Example of a Stakeholder Matrix

Benefits of Stakeholder Mapping

- **Improves decision-making**: Ensures that all relevant perspectives are considered.

- **Enhances communication**: Helps tailor messages to the right audience.
- **Facilitates engagement**: Encourages active involvement from key stakeholders.
- **Identifies risks**: Helps in anticipating potential opposition or challenges.

Stakeholder mapping is a dynamic process and should be revisited regularly throughout the lifecycle of a policy or project to ensure continued alignment and support.

When conducting stakeholder mapping, it's essential to identify both opportunities and barriers that can impact the success of your policy, project or initiative. Understanding these factors will help you devise effective strategies to maximize the positive impact and mitigate potential challenges. Here's how you can approach identifying opportunities and barriers in stakeholder mapping:

Identifying Opportunities

1. Leverage Influential Stakeholders

- **Support and advocacy**: High-influence stakeholders who are supportive of your initiative can advocate for it, helping to gain broader acceptance and facilitate smoother implementation.
- **Resource mobilization**: Stakeholders with significant influence might provide financial, human or technical resources that can be critical for success.

2. Align Interests

- **Shared goals**: Identifying stakeholders with aligned or complementary interests can create partnerships and coalitions that strengthen the initiative.
- **Mutual benefits**: Highlighting how stakeholders can benefit from the success of the initiative can increase their engagement and commitment.

3. Increase Participation and Buy-in

- Involving stakeholders in decision-making: Providing stakeholders with a role in the decision-making process can increase their sense of ownership and reduce resistance.
- Improving transparency and communication: Open communication channels can build trust and ensure that stakeholders feel their concerns are being heard and addressed.

4. Identify Champions

- **Influence networks**: Some stakeholders can act as champions or ambassadors for the initiative within their networks, helping to spread positive messaging and garner additional support.
- **Grassroots support**: Engaging with community leaders or grassroots organizations can create a strong base of support, especially for initiatives that directly affect local populations.

Identifying Barriers

1. Resistance from Powerful Stakeholders

- **Opposition to change**: High-influence stakeholders who oppose the initiative can create significant roadblocks, such as lobbying against it, withholding resources or mobilizing public opinion against it.
- **Conflicting interests**: Stakeholders with interests that conflict with the initiative's goals may actively work to undermine it.

2. Lack of Stakeholder Engagement

- **Disengagement**: Stakeholders with low interest but high influence may be disengaged, which could lead to a lack of support or even passive resistance.
- **Communication gaps**: Poor communication with stakeholders can lead to misunderstandings, misalignment or lack of awareness about the initiative's goals and benefits.

3. Resource Constraints

- **Limited resources**: Some stakeholders may have a high interest but lack the resources (time, money, personnel) to fully engage or support the initiative, which could limit its effectiveness.
- **Competing priorities**: Stakeholders might prioritize other initiatives over yours, especially if they are stretched thin or have limited capacity.

4. Cultural and Social Barriers

- **Cultural misalignment**: Differences in values, beliefs or cultural norms between stakeholders and the initiative can lead to resistance or misinterpretation of the initiative's intentions.
- **Social dynamics**: Existing power dynamics or social hierarchies within stakeholder groups may complicate engagement and collaboration efforts.

5. Regulatory and Legal Constraints

- **Legal barriers**: Existing laws or regulations may limit the ability of certain stakeholders to engage with or support the initiative.
- **Bureaucratic resistance**: Government agencies or other regulatory bodies might resist changes that disrupt established procedures or challenge existing authority.

Strategies to Address Opportunities and Barriers

1. Engage Early and Often

- **Proactive communication**: Regular, transparent communication with stakeholders can help address concerns early and build trust.
- **Inclusion in planning**: Involve key stakeholders in the planning stages to ensure their needs and concerns are addressed from the outset.

2. Tailor Engagement Approaches

- **Customized strategies**: Develop specific strategies for engaging different stakeholder groups based on their level of influence, interest and potential barriers.
- **Flexible engagement**: Be adaptable in your approach, ready to adjust strategies as stakeholder positions or external conditions change.

3. Build Alliances

- **Coalition building**: Form alliances with stakeholders who have aligned interests or who can help neutralize opposition from more resistant stakeholders.
- **Collaborative solutions**: Work with stakeholders to co-create solutions that address their concerns and reduce barriers to engagement.

4. Leverage Positive Stakeholders

- **Empower champions**: Give influential, supportive stakeholders a platform to promote the initiative and help sway others.
- **Highlight successes**: Showcase early wins or benefits of the initiative to build momentum and demonstrate value to hesitant stakeholders.

5. Mitigate Resistance

- **Address concerns**: Engage directly with resistant stakeholders to understand their concerns and work collaboratively to find mutually acceptable solutions.

- **Minimize impact**: Where resistance cannot be fully mitigated, minimize the impact by focusing on other areas where support is stronger.

By carefully identifying and addressing opportunities and barriers through stakeholder mapping, you can create more effective strategies that lead to successful policy implementation or project completion.

Mobilizing Financial Resources

Mobilizing financial resources is a critical component of successful policy-making. Securing adequate funding ensures that policies can be effectively implemented, monitored and sustained. Here's how you can approach the process of mobilizing financial resources in policy-making:

1. Identifying Financial Needs

- **Cost estimation**: Accurately estimate the costs associated with policy implementation, including infrastructure, staffing, technology, monitoring and evaluation.
- **Budget planning**: Develop a detailed budget that outlines the financial requirements for each phase of the policy, from design to full implementation.

2. Identifying Funding Sources

- **Government budgets**
    - **National and local budgets**: Seek allocations from government budgets at both national and local levels. This may involve working with relevant ministries, departments or local authorities.
    - **Reallocation**: Advocate for reallocating existing funds from less critical areas to support the new policy.
    - **Earmarked taxes or levies**: Propose the introduction of specific taxes or levies dedicated to funding the policy.
- **International Funding**
    - **Multilateral and bilateral aid**: Engage with international organizations such as the World Bank, IMF or UN agencies, as well as bilateral donors, to secure grants, loans or technical assistance.
    - **Development funds**: Access development funds targeted at specific sectors like health, education or environmental sustainability.
- **Private sector involvement**
    - **Public-Private Partnerships (PPPs)**: Establish partnerships with private companies that can co-fund or manage aspects of the policy implementation.

    - **Corporate Social Responsibility (CSR)**: Leverage CSR initiatives where companies fund or support social or environmental projects aligned with their corporate values.
- **Philanthropic organizations and NGOs**
    - **Grants and donations**: Approach foundations, NGOs and philanthropic organizations that align with the policy's objectives for financial support.
    - **Social impact bonds**: Explore social impact bonds, where private investors fund policy initiatives with the expectation of returns based on successful outcomes.
- **Community and grassroots funding**
    - **Crowd funding**: Use crowd funding platforms to raise small amounts from a large number of people, particularly for policies with strong public appeal.
    - **Local fundraising**: Engage communities directly through fundraising events, local campaigns or voluntary contributions.

3. Making the Case for Investment

- **Cost-Benefit analysis**: Conduct a cost-benefit analysis to demonstrate the long-term economic, social or environmental benefits of the policy compared to its costs.
- **Return On Investment (ROI)**: Highlight potential ROI, particularly for private sector and philanthropic stakeholders, by illustrating how the policy can lead to positive social outcomes or market opportunities.
- **Alignment with donor priorities**: Ensure that the policy aligns with the goals and priorities of potential donors or funders, emphasizing shared objectives.

4. Building Strategic Alliances

- **Coalition building**: Form coalitions with other stakeholders, such as NGOs, industry groups or international organizations, to collectively advocate for resource mobilization.
- **Advocacy and lobbying**: Engage in advocacy and lobbying efforts to influence budget decisions and attract funding from government and private sources.

5. Developing a Financial Sustainability Plan

- **Diversification of funding**: Avoid reliance on a single funding source by diversifying funding streams to include a mix of government, private sector and international resources.
- **Long-term planning**: Develop a long-term financial plan that includes provisions for ongoing maintenance, scaling or expansion of the policy.
- **Contingency planning**: Include contingency plans for potential shortfalls or delays in funding, ensuring that critical aspects of the policy can still be implemented.

6. Transparent financial management

- **Accountability mechanisms**: Establish transparent financial management practices, including regular audits, to ensure that funds are used effectively and efficiently.
- **Reporting and evaluation**: Provide regular reports to funders and stakeholders, demonstrating how funds are being used and the progress being made toward policy goals.

7. Monitoring and Adapting

- **Ongoing monitoring**: Continuously monitor the financial health of the policy implementation process to identify any gaps or opportunities for additional funding.
- **Flexible financing**: Be prepared to adapt financing strategies in response to changing circumstances, such as new funding opportunities or shifts in policy priorities.

8. Communication and Outreach

- **Engaging the public**: Use media and communication strategies to build public support for the policy, which can, in turn, create pressure on decision-makers to allocate funds.
- **Highlighting successes**: Publicize successful milestones to build confidence among existing and potential funders, demonstrating that the policy is on track and delivering results.

Mobilizing financial resources in policy-making is an ongoing process that requires careful planning, strategic engagement with stakeholders and a strong case for investment. By diversifying funding sources and maintaining transparency, policymakers can secure the necessary financial support to ensure the success of their initiatives.

Dealing with policy in coherences: Identifying contradistinctions and challenges in policy implementation

Dealing with policy in coherences involves identifying contradictions, overlaps or gaps in policies that can hinder effective implementation. Addressing these issues is crucial for ensuring that policies achieve their intended outcomes. Here's a guide on how to identify and manage these challenges:

1. Identifying Policy in Coherences

A. Contradictions between policies

- **Inconsistent objectives**: When different policies have goals that conflict with each other, leading to confusion and inefficiency.

  Example: A policy promoting industrial growth might contradict environmental policies aimed at reducing emissions.

- **Regulatory overlaps**: Multiple policies or regulations addressing the same issue in different ways, creating redundancy and confusion.

  Example: Separate regulations on land use from different agencies that impose conflicting requirements on developers.

- **Policy Gaps**: Areas where no policy exists, leading to issues being unaddressed or poorly managed.

  Example: A lack of clear guidelines on emerging technologies like AI, creating uncertainty and inconsistent practices.

B. Implementation Challenges

- **Resource misalignment**: Policies may require resources (financial, human, technical) that are not available or are misallocated.

  Example: A policy demanding extensive data collection without providing the necessary infrastructure or training.

- **Institutional silos**: Different government agencies or departments working in isolation, leading to poor coordination and conflicting actions.

  Example: Health and education departments working on overlapping social programs without coordination, leading to duplicative efforts.

- **Legal and bureaucratic barriers**: Existing laws, regulations or bureaucratic processes that obstruct the smooth implementation of new policies.

  Example: Rigid procurement rules delaying the rollout of a new government-funded program.

C. Stakeholder Opposition

- **Resistance from affected groups**: Stakeholders who perceive a policy as harmful to their interests may resist its implementation.

  Example: Businesses lobbying against labor regulations they believe will increase operational costs.

- **Lack of public support**: Policies that do not align with public opinion or cultural norms may face resistance, leading to poor compliance.

  Example: A public health policy mandating vaccinations in a community with low trust in government.

2. Addressing policy in Coherences

A. Conducting a Coherence Review

- **Policy analysis**: Systematically review existing policies to identify contradictions, overlaps and gaps. This can involve:
- **Comparative analysis**: Compare new and existing policies to identify conflicting objectives or requirements.
- **Consultations**: Engage with stakeholders, including government agencies, experts and the public, to gather insights on potential in coherences.
- **Impact assessment**: Evaluate the potential impacts of identified in coherences on policy outcomes, efficiency and public trust.

B. Improving Coordination and Communication

- **Inter-agency collaboration**: Foster better coordination between different government departments or agencies to align policies and reduce overlaps.
- **Joint committees**: Establish inter-agency committees or task forces to ensure consistent policy implementation across sectors.
- **Integrated policy frameworks**: Develop comprehensive frameworks that integrate policies across different sectors, ensuring they work together toward common goals.

  Example: A sustainable development framework that aligns economic, social and environmental policies.

C. Enhancing Stakeholder Engagement

- **Inclusive policy making**: Involve a broad range of stakeholders in the policymaking process to identify potential conflicts and build consensus.

- **Public consultations**: Hold public consultations or town halls to gather input from affected communities and address concerns early.
- **Conflict resolution mechanisms**: Establish mechanisms for resolving disputes between stakeholders that arise from policy in coherences.
- **Mediation**: Use third-party mediators to resolve conflicts between stakeholders with opposing views.

D. Revising and Harmonizing Policies

- **Policy amendments**: Revise or amend policies to remove contradictions and ensure they are aligned with overarching goals.

  Example: Amending industrial policies to incorporate stricter environmental standards in line with climate change commitments.
- **Regulatory harmonization**: Standardize regulations across different sectors or jurisdictions to reduce confusion and ensure consistent implementation.

  Example: Harmonizing building codes across regions to ensure uniform safety standards.

E. Strengthening Institutional Capacities

- **Capacity building**: Enhance the capabilities of institutions responsible for policy implementation, ensuring they can effectively manage complexities and challenges.
- **Training**: Provide training for public officials on policy coherence, inter-agency collaboration and stakeholder engagement.
- **Resource allocation**: Ensure that institutions have the necessary resources to implement policies effectively, including financial, technical and human resources.

  Example: Allocating budgetary resources to support the coordination of multi-sectoral policies.

F. Continuous Monitoring and Evaluation

- **Monitoring systems**: Establish robust monitoring systems to track policy implementation and identify any emerging in coherences or challenges.
- **Real-time data**: Use real-time data and feedback mechanisms to adjust policies as needed during implementation.
- **Policy evaluation**: Regularly evaluate the effectiveness of policies in achieving their goals and address any in coherences that may have arisen.

- **Feedback loops**: Create feedback loops that allow for continuous improvement of policies based on evaluation results.

3. Managing Policy in Coherences in Practice

- **Adaptive policy design**: Design policies that are flexible and can be adjusted in response to new information or changing circumstances. This approach allows for continuous alignment and coherence.
- **Strategic prioritization**: When faced with multiple in coherences, prioritize addressing those that have the most significant impact on policy outcomes or stakeholder trust.
- **Political leadership and commitment**: Strong political leadership is crucial for driving the alignment of policies, especially when dealing with entrenched interests or institutional inertia.

By proactively identifying and addressing policy in coherences, policymakers can enhance the effectiveness of their initiatives, ensure smoother implementation and build public trust in government actions.

5

Influencing Policy Change Through Generating Evidence: The Role of Policy Research

Policy research plays a critical role in influencing policy change by generating robust evidence that can guide decision-making processes. The use of evidence is crucial in ensuring that policies are both effective and appropriate to address specific issues. Evidence-based policy-making relies on credible, relevant and timely research that helps identify problems, evaluate potential solutions and forecast the impacts of various policy options.

Role of Policy Research in Generating Evidence

1. **Identification of issues:** Policy research begins with identifying key issues or challenges that require policy intervention. This involves conducting systematic research to understand the scope, scale and nature of the problem. For example, research on gender disparities in agricultural labor in India may highlight specific barriers women face, such as lack of access to resources or discriminatory practices.
2. **Data collection and analysis:** Gathering quantitative and qualitative data is essential for building a comprehensive understanding of the issue. For instance, data collection may involve surveys, interviews, case studies and secondary data analysis to capture diverse perspectives and experiences. This data provides a solid foundation for analyzing the problem's root causes and identifying the affected population.
3. **Evaluation of policy options:** Policy research involves evaluating various policy options to determine their potential effectiveness. Researchers analyze different approaches by considering factors such as cost, feasibility, scalability and potential impact on stakeholders. For example, assessing different subsidy models for women farmers can reveal which is most likely to improve their economic status while being financially sustainable.

4. **Forecasting and impact assessment:** Predicting the potential outcomes of policy decisions is a critical step in influencing policy change. Using models, simulations and scenario analyses, researchers can provide evidence on the likely impacts of various policy interventions. This evidence helps policymakers anticipate both intended and unintended consequences, allowing for better planning and risk mitigation.
5. **Advocacy and communication:** The ultimate goal of policy research is to communicate findings effectively to policymakers and stakeholders. This involves translating complex data and analysis into clear, actionable recommendations. Research institutions, think tanks and non-governmental organizations often play a key role in advocating for policy changes by presenting evidence in a way that resonates with decision-makers and the public.

Analyzing the Usefulness and Appropriateness Of Evidence

The effectiveness of policy research in influencing change depends on the quality and relevance of the evidence produced. High-quality evidence is characterized by reliability, validity, transparency and reproducibility. To avoid plagiarism and maintain the integrity of research, proper referencing and citation of all sources are critical. Moreover, the appropriateness of evidence depends on its alignment with the policy context, cultural relevance and its ability to address the needs and priorities of the target population.

In evaluating the usefulness of evidence, policymakers must consider:

- **Relevance:** Does the evidence address the specific policy question or challenge at hand?
- **Timeliness:** Is the evidence up-to-date and reflective of current conditions?
- **Credibility:** Are the data sources reliable and are the research methods rigorous?
- **Accessibility:** Is the evidence presented in a way that is understandable and actionable for policymakers?

By meeting these criteria, policy research can provide a solid foundation for advocating for meaningful policy changes that improve social, economic and environmental outcomes.

Using Evidence in Policy Advocacy

Using evidence in policy advocacy involves systematically gathering, analyzing and presenting data to influence policy decisions and promote desired changes.

Evidence-based advocacy ensures that arguments are grounded in reliable and relevant information, which increases the credibility and effectiveness of advocacy efforts. The process involves several key components:

1. **Evidence collection and analysis:** The foundation of evidence-based advocacy is the collection and rigorous analysis of data. This may involve both quantitative data (such as statistics, surveys and economic data) and qualitative data (such as case studies, interviews and focus group discussions). Evidence should be robust, transparent and derived from credible sources to withstand scrutiny by policymakers and other stakeholders.
2. **Tailoring evidence to the audience:** Different audiences, such as government officials, legislators, the media and the public, require different types of evidence. For example, policymakers may be more responsive to cost-benefit analyses and empirical data that demonstrate the effectiveness of a proposed policy, while the general public may be more engaged by personal narratives and human-interest stories that illustrate the real-world impact of an issue.
3. **Presenting evidence effectively:** To influence policy decisions, evidence must be communicated clearly and compellingly. This can involve creating policy briefs, fact sheets, info-graphics, reports and presentations that distill complex information into accessible and actionable insights. Visualizing data and using storytelling techniques can also enhance the persuasiveness of evidence.
4. **Monitoring and evaluation:** Continuous monitoring and evaluation are essential to assess the impact of advocacy efforts and refine strategies as needed. This involves tracking changes in policy discussions, media coverage, public opinion and policy outcomes. Evidence from these evaluations can be used to adjust advocacy tactics and strengthen future efforts.
5. **Building credibility and rust:** Evidence-based advocacy builds credibility and trust with decision-makers by demonstrating a commitment to transparency, rigor and accountability. When advocacy organizations consistently use high-quality evidence and ethical research practices, they establish themselves as reliable sources of information, increasing the likelihood that their recommendations will be taken seriously by policymakers.

Policy advocacy is a strategic process that uses evidence to influence policy decisions and promote changes that benefit society. To be effective, advocates must understand their audience, identify the most influential channels, build alliances and engage policy champions. Evidence-based advocacy ensures that arguments are grounded in reliable data and research, increasing the credibility and impact of the advocacy efforts.

Understanding your Audience

Understanding the audience is crucial in tailoring messages and strategies for effective policy advocacy. Different stakeholders, including policymakers, government officials, civil society organizations and the general public, have diverse interests, needs and levels of influence. Advocates must analyze the audience's values, concerns and preferred communication styles. For example, while policymakers may respond to cost-benefit analyses and statistical evidence, the general public might be more engaged by personal stories and visual data.

Analyzing Channels of Influence

Channels of influence refer to the platforms and pathways through which advocacy messages reach key decision-makers. These can include media outlets, social media, direct communication (*e.g.*, meetings, letters), public forums and legislative hearings. Selecting the appropriate channels is crucial for ensuring that evidence-based messages reach the intended audience effectively. Advocates should analyze which channels are most trusted and accessible to their target audience and focus on using those to disseminate their evidence. For instance, when advocating for policy changes in agricultural labor rights, advocates might utilize policy briefs, webinars, or social media campaigns to reach both policymakers and the public.

Creating Alliances

Building alliances with like-minded organizations, stakeholders and interest groups can strengthen advocacy efforts. Alliances can amplify advocacy messages, provide access to additional resources and enhance credibility. Collaborative networks allow for pooling expertise, sharing evidence and creating a unified front to address policy challenges. For example, forming coalitions with farmer organizations, women's groups and research institutions can be crucial in advocating for gender equity in agriculture. These alliances increase visibility, facilitate the sharing of data and create a stronger, more persuasive case for policy change.

Identifying Policy Champions

Policy champions are individuals who have the influence, authority and commitment to drive policy changes. They can be legislators, government officials, community leaders, or influential public figures. Identifying and engaging policy champions is vital for advancing advocacy goals because they can use their positions to promote the proposed changes, provide access to decision-making arenas and mobilize support from other stakeholders. For example, a member of parliament who has a strong interest in gender equity issues could be a valuable ally in pushing for policies that support women agricultural laborers.

Defining Goals and Objectives of Policy Change and Developing Advocacy Messages

In the realm of policy advocacy, defining clear goals and objectives and crafting effective advocacy messages are essential steps for achieving meaningful policy change. These steps help to ensure that advocacy efforts are strategic, focused and aligned with desired outcomes.

Defining Goals and Objectives of Policy Change

1. **Setting clear goals:** Goals are broad, overarching aims that an advocacy campaign seeks to achieve. They provide the overall direction and purpose of the advocacy effort, such as enhancing environmental sustainability, improving public health outcomes, or promoting social equity. Goals should be visionary, but they must also be realistic and attainable within the context of the political, social and economic environment.
2. **Establishing specific objectives:** Objectives are the Specific, Measurable, Achievable, Relevant and Time-bound (SMART) steps that outline the path to achieving the broader goal. They translate the general aim into concrete actions and milestones.
3. **Prioritizing issues:** Effective advocacy requires prioritizing the most critical issues based on factors such as urgency, potential impact and political feasibility. Advocates must consider the current policy environment, stakeholder interests and available resources to identify which issues offer the best opportunities for advancing their goals. This prioritization process ensures that advocacy efforts are both strategic and impactful.

Developing Advocacy Messages

1. **Crafting persuasive messages:** Advocacy messages must be clear, compelling and tailored to the specific audience. They should articulate the problem, propose a solution and specify the action required from the audience. Effective messages often incorporate a combination of factual information and emotional appeal to persuade the audience to support the desired policy change. For instance, messages advocating for clean air regulations might combine statistics on health impacts with personal stories of individuals affected by pollution.
2. **Adapting messages for different audiences:** Different audiences, such as policymakers, community members, media and donors, have varying interests, values and communication preferences. Tailoring messages to resonate with each audience is crucial. Policymakers may be more receptive to messages that highlight evidence-based outcomes and cost-effectiveness, while community members may respond better to stories that emphasize social justice or personal impact. Customizing messages ensures that they are relevant and engaging for each group.
3. **Using evidence to strengthen messages:** Incorporating credible evidence, such as data, research findings and expert testimonials, strengthens advocacy messages by enhancing their legitimacy and persuasiveness. Evidence-based messages help build trust with decision-makers and stakeholders, demonstrating that the proposed policy change is grounded in reliable information. For example, presenting statistical data on the economic benefits of gender equality in the workforce can help persuade policymakers to support gender-focused policies.
4. **Balancing emotional and rational appeals:** Effective advocacy messages often balance emotional and rational appeals. Emotional appeals can engage an audience's values, empathy and sense of justice, while rational appeals provide logical arguments supported by data and evidence. For example, an advocacy campaign for improved maternal healthcare services might use personal narratives to highlight the human impact of inadequate care, alongside data demonstrating the cost-effectiveness of proposed improvements.

Developing Advocacy Messages: Policy Papers, Policy Briefs and Good Practice Notes

Developing effective advocacy messages is a crucial aspect of influencing policy change. Key tools in this process include policy papers, policy briefs and good practice notes. Each tool serves a specific purpose and audience and using them effectively requires a clear understanding of their characteristics and best practices.

Policy Papers

Policy papers are detailed documents that analyze specific policy issues, present evidence and provide comprehensive recommendations. They are often used to inform policymakers, researchers and stakeholders about complex problems and potential solutions.

Characteristics

- **In-depth analysis:** Policy papers provide a thorough examination of a policy issue, including background information, data analysis and evidence-based arguments.
- **Detailed recommendations:** They offer specific recommendations for policy changes or actions based on the analysis.
- **Target audience:** Policy papers are usually aimed at policymakers, experts and academics who require detailed information to make informed decisions.

Best Practices

- **Clarity and structure:** Organize the paper with a clear structure, including an introduction, background, analysis, recommendations and conclusion.
- **Evidence-based:** Support arguments with credible data, research findings and case studies.
- **Accessibility:** Use clear language and avoid jargon to make the paper accessible to a broader audience if necessary.

Policy Briefs

Policy briefs are concise documents designed to present key information and recommendations in a clear and accessible format. They are intended to quickly inform and persuade policymakers and other stakeholders.

Characteristics

- **Concise and focused:** Policy briefs are typically 2-4 pages long, summarizing the main points and recommendations of a policy issue.
- **Action-oriented:** They focus on actionable recommendations and practical steps that policymakers can take.

- **Target audience:** Policymakers, advocates and the general public who need a quick overview of an issue.

Best Practices

- **Clear and direct:** Use straightforward language and focus on the most important information.
- **Engaging design:** Incorporate visuals such as charts, graphs and infographics to make the brief more engaging and easier to understand.
- **Call to action:** Clearly articulate the desired action or policy change.

Good Practice Notes

Good practice notes provide practical guidance and examples of successful approaches to specific policy issues. They are designed to share best practices and lessons learned from various experiences.

Characteristics

- **Practical guidance:** They offer practical advice based on real-world examples and experiences.
- **Case studies:** Often include case studies or examples that illustrate successful implementation of practices.
- **Target audience:** Practitioners, policymakers and organizations seeking to implement effective strategies or improve their practices.

Best Practices

- **Relevant examples:** Use relevant and recent examples to illustrate good practices and lessons learned.
- **Practical tips:** Provide actionable tips and recommendations that can be easily implemented.
- **Clear formatting:** Use a clear format with headings, bullet points and summaries to enhance readability.

Good Practices in Influencing Policies: Organizing Policy Dialogues

Organizing policy dialogues is an effective strategy for influencing policies and fostering collaborative discussions among stakeholders. These dialogues create platforms for exchanging ideas, building consensus and developing actionable solutions to policy issues. Good practices in organizing policy dialogues ensure that these events are productive, inclusive and impactful.

Key Good Practices in Organizing Policy Dialogues

1. Define Clear Objectives

- **Purpose:** Establish the specific goals of the policy dialogue, such as exploring policy options, gaining stakeholder input, or building support for a proposed change.
- **Outcomes:** Define the desired outcomes, such as generating recommendations, identifying common ground, or outlining next steps for advocacy.

2. Engage Relevant Stakeholders

- **Diverse participants:** Invite a broad range of stakeholders, including policymakers, experts, affected communities, advocacy groups and the public. Ensuring diverse representation helps capture various perspectives and fosters more comprehensive discussions.
- **Pre-dialogue engagement:** Engage stakeholders before the event through surveys, interviews, or preliminary meetings to understand their interests, concerns and expectations.

3. Prepare Thoroughly

- **Agenda:** Develop a clear and structured agenda that outlines the topics to be discussed, the sequence of activities and the time allocated for each session.
- **Background materials:** Provide participants with relevant background materials, such as research findings, policy briefs and case studies, well in advance of the dialogue to ensure informed discussions.

4. Facilitate Inclusive and Constructive Discussions

- **Neutral facilitation:** Employ a skilled facilitator who can manage discussions impartially, encourage participation from all stakeholders and address conflicts constructively.
- **Interactive formats:** Use interactive formats such as breakout sessions, roundtable discussions and Q&A sessions to engage participants and facilitate deeper exploration of issues.

5. Document and Follow up

- **Record proceedings:** Document key discussions, decisions and recommendations made during the dialogue. This can include taking detailed minutes, recording sessions and summarizing key points.

- **Action plan:** Develop a follow-up action plan based on the dialogue outcomes, including next steps, responsibilities and timelines. Share the results with participants and relevant stakeholders to maintain momentum and accountability.

6. Evaluate and Improve

- **Feedback:** Collect feedback from participants on the effectiveness of the dialogue, including what worked well and areas for improvement.
- **Continuous improvement:** Use the feedback to refine future policy dialogues, ensuring that each event builds on previous experiences and better meets the needs of stakeholders.

Policy Engagement Strategy: Engaging with Policymakers Through Various Mechanisms

A robust policy engagement strategy involves multiple approaches to effectively interact with policymakers and influence policy outcomes. These approaches include leveraging the experiences of Governmental Organizations (GOs) and Non-Governmental Organizations (NGOs), participating in policy working groups and advisory panels and utilizing committees. Understanding these mechanisms helps in crafting strategies that can enhance advocacy efforts and drive meaningful policy change.

Engaging with Policymakers

1. Experiences of Governmental and Non-Governmental Organizations

Governmental Organizations (GOs): GOs often engage with policymakers through formal channels such as policy briefs, reports and official consultations. They can leverage their authority and resources to shape policy discussions and outcomes. For example, government departments may use their data and expertise to propose new regulations or amendments to existing policies.

- **Non-Governmental Organizations (NGOs):** NGOs typically engage with policymakers through advocacy campaigns, lobbying and public awareness efforts. They may use grassroots mobilization, media campaigns and direct meetings with legislators to influence policy. NGOs often bring forward the perspectives of marginalized communities and can provide valuable evidence and case studies to support their advocacy.

2. Policy Working Groups

Policy working groups are collaborative forums where stakeholders, including policymakers, experts and interest groups, come together to discuss specific policy issues and develop recommendations.

- **Role:** Working groups facilitate in-depth analysis and discussion of complex policy matters. They allow for the exchange of diverse perspectives and expertise, leading to more informed and balanced policy recommendations.
- **Example:** An example of a policy working group might be a task force on climate change, where environmentalists, scientists and industry representatives collaborate to propose actionable climate policies.

3. Advisory Panels

Advisory panels consist of experts and stakeholders who provide guidance and recommendations to policymakers on specific issues or programs.

- **Role:** Panels offer specialized knowledge and insights that can help shape policy decisions. They are often used to review and provide feedback on policy proposals or to assess the impact of existing policies.
- **Example:** A health advisory panel might provide recommendations on public health strategies and interventions based on the latest research and trends.

4. Use of Committees

Committees are formal bodies within legislative or governmental structures that review, discuss and make decisions on policy matters.

- **Role:** Committees play a crucial role in the legislative process by scrutinizing bills, holding hearings and gathering evidence from various stakeholders. They are essential for shaping and refining policy proposals before they are enacted into law.
- **Example:** A parliamentary committee on education might hold hearings with educators, parents and students to gather input on proposed education reforms.

Use of Media for Influencing Policies

Media plays a critical role in influencing public policy by shaping public opinion, providing information and fostering dialogue between policymakers and the public. The effective use of media can amplify advocacy efforts, bring attention to policy issues and drive policy changes.

Traditional Media

1. Newspapers

- **Role:** Newspapers offer a platform for in-depth reporting and analysis on policy issues. They can influence public opinion and highlight specific policy concerns through editorials, news articles and investigative journalism.
- **Strategies:**
  - **Op-eds and letters to the editor:** Publishing op-eds and letters can provide a forum for advocates to present arguments and recommendations directly to the readership.
  - **Feature Stories:** Detailed feature stories can raise awareness about policy issues by providing comprehensive coverage and human-interest angles.

2. Television and Radio

- **Role:** Television and radio reach a broad audience and are effective in disseminating information quickly. They can influence public perception and policymaking through news reports, interviews and public service announcements.
- **Strategies**
  - **News segments and interviews:** Securing coverage in news segments or participating in interviews can help spotlight issues and advocate for specific policy changes.
  - **Public Service Announcements (PSAs):** PSAs can be used to promote awareness of critical issues and mobilize public support for policy initiatives.

Digital media

1. Online news Outlets and Blogs

- **Role:** Digital media, including online news sites and blogs, provide real-time information and allow for detailed discussions of policy issues. They offer a platform for diverse voices and viewpoints.
- **Strategies:**
  - **Guest articles and blog posts:** Writing guest articles or blog posts can contribute to ongoing discussions and influence policy by providing expert analysis and commentary.

- **Online campaigns:** Launching digital campaigns can drive engagement and mobilize support for policy changes through petitions, calls to action and awareness-raising content.

2. Social Media

- **Role:** Social media platforms facilitate real-time interaction and engagement, making them powerful tools for advocacy and policy influence. They enable the rapid dissemination of information and mobilization of public opinion.
- **Strategies:**
    - **Hashtag campaigns:** Creating and promoting hashtags can focus attention on specific issues and encourage public discourse.
    - **Influencer collaboration:** Partnering with influencers can amplify messages and reach broader audiences, increasing the visibility of policy issues.

Using Information and Communication Technologies (ICTs) for Influencing Policies

Information and Communication Technologies (ICTs) have become essential tools in influencing public policy. They enable advocacy groups, researchers and policymakers to gather, analyze and disseminate information more efficiently, engage with stakeholders and mobilize public support. The strategic use of ICTs can enhance advocacy efforts, streamline policy processes and facilitate more informed decision-making.

Key Uses of ICTs in Policy Influence

1. Data collection and analysis

- **Role:** ICTs facilitate the collection and analysis of large volumes of data, which can provide valuable insights into policy issues and inform decision-making.
- **Tools and Techniques**

    a) **Surveys and polls:** Online surveys and polls enable the collection of public opinion data and stakeholder feedback on policy issues.

    b) **Data visualization:** Tools such as graphs, charts and interactive maps help present complex data in an accessible and engaging format, making it easier to understand and communicate findings.

2. Information Dissemination

- **Role:** ICTs help disseminate information quickly and widely, reaching diverse audiences and raising awareness about policy issues.
- **Tools and Techniques**

  a) **Websites and blogs:** Creating and maintaining websites and blogs allows for the publication of detailed information, research findings and advocacy messages.

  b) **Email campaigns:** Email newsletters and campaigns can inform stakeholders about policy updates, upcoming events and calls to action.

3. Engagement and Advocacy

- **Role:** ICTs enable direct engagement with policymakers, stakeholders and the public, fostering dialogue and building support for policy initiatives.
- **Tools and Techniques**

  a) **Social media:** Platforms such as twitter, facebook and linkedin facilitate real-time communication, mobilize public opinion and amplify advocacy messages.

  b) **Online petitions:** Digital petitions allow individuals to express support or opposition to specific policies, demonstrating public sentiment and influencing policymakers.

4. Collaboration and Networking

- **Role:** ICTs support collaboration and networking among advocacy groups, researchers and policymakers, enhancing collective efforts to influence policy.
- **Tools and techniques**

  a) **Virtual meetings and webinars:** Online conferencing tools enable remote meetings and webinars, allowing for real-time discussions and information sharing among stakeholders.

  b) **Collaborative platforms:** Tools like Google Docs and Slack facilitate joint research, document sharing and communication among advocacy teams and policy experts.

5. Monitoring and Evaluation

- **Role:** ICTs assist in monitoring and evaluating policy impacts, providing feedback on the effectiveness of policy interventions and advocacy strategies.

- **Tools and Techniques**
  a) **Analytics and tracking:** Using analytics tools to track website traffic, social media engagement and email campaign performance helps assess the reach and impact of advocacy efforts.
  b) **Feedback mechanisms:** Online feedback forms and surveys gather input from stakeholders and the public on policy implementation and outcomes.

Use of Social Media for Influencing Policies

Social media has become a pivotal tool in modern advocacy, offering a platform for influencing public policy by shaping public opinion, mobilizing grassroots support and facilitating direct communication with policymakers. Its widespread use and rapid dissemination capabilities make it an effective medium for driving policy change and engaging with various stakeholders.

Key uses of Social Media in Policy Influence

1. Raising Awareness

a) Role: Social media platforms, such as twitter, face-book and instagram, provide avenues for raising awareness about policy issues and reaching a large audience quickly.

b) Strategies:

- **Campaigns and hash-tags:** Using hash-tags and running social media campaigns can spotlight specific issues and generate widespread discussion. For example, the Me Too movement used social media to bring attention to sexual harassment and influence policy changes.
- **Educational content:** Sharing info-graphics, articles and videos can help educate the public and policymakers about important issues and potential solutions.

2. Engaging and Mobilizing the Public

a) Role: Social media facilitates engagement with the public, encouraging participation in advocacy efforts and influencing policy discussions.

b) Strategies

- **Calls to action:** Posting calls to action, such as signing petitions, contacting legislators, or attending rallies, can mobilize public support and create pressure for policy change.
- **Interactive features:** Utilizing social media tools like polls, Q&A sessions and live broadcasts enables real-time interaction and feedback from the community.

3. Shaping Public Opinion

a) **Role:** Social media platforms influence public opinion by providing a space for discourse and the dissemination of information.

b) **Strategies**

- **Influencer partnerships:** Collaborating with social media influencers and thought leaders can amplify advocacy messages and reach broader audiences, thereby shaping public perception on policy issues.
- **Storytelling:** Sharing personal stories and experiences can humanize policy issues and make them more relatable, thereby influencing public attitudes and policy preferences.

4. Monitoring and Responding to Policy Developments

a) **Role:** Social media provides a means to track policy developments, public sentiment and the activities of policymakers in real-time.

b) **Strategies**

- **Real-time updates:** Following social media updates from policymakers and news sources helps stay informed about policy changes and emerging issues.
- **Feedback collection:** Analyzing engagement metrics and public feedback on social media can provide insights into the effectiveness of advocacy efforts and guide future strategies.

5. Advocacy and Campaigning

a) **Role:** Social media is a key platform for conducting advocacy campaigns and rallying support for policy changes.

b) **Strategies:**

- **Strategic posting:** Timing posts around significant events or policy announcements can maximize visibility and impact.
- **Community building:** Creating and nurturing online communities around specific issues can build solidarity and foster collective action.

6

Global Experience with Agricultural Extension Policies

Agricultural extension services are critical for the dissemination of knowledge, technologies and innovations among farmers, leading to improved agricultural productivity, sustainability and livelihoods. Different countries have adopted varied approaches to extension policies, reflecting their unique socio-economic, political and agro-ecological contexts. Here's an overview of extension policies in different regions:

1. **United States:** In the United States, the Cooperative Extension Service, established under the Smith-Lever Act of 1914, is a nationwide, publicly funded network that connects land-grant universities with local communities. It provides educational programs, resources and advisory services to farmers, ranchers and rural residents. The U.S. model emphasizes partnerships between federal, state and local governments, as well as with the private sector, to deliver extension services.
2. **India:** India has a diverse and decentralized extension system comprising public, private and Non-Governmental Organizations (NGOs). The National Mission on Agricultural Extension and Technology (NMAET) is the central government's flagship program that focuses on agricultural extension, including farmer capacity building, technology dissemination and knowledge management. Despite this, challenges such as inadequate funding, limited reach and poor coordination across agencies persist, leading to calls for reform and more innovative approaches like Information and Communication Technology (ICT) integration.
3. **Brazil:** Brazil's extension services are provided by both public and private sectors. The Brazilian Agricultural Research Corporation (EMBRAPA) plays a significant role in research and extension. The country's extension policy focuses on sustainable agriculture, agro-ecology and the inclusion of family farmers. Decentralization and the involvement of municipal governments and local organizations are key features, which help tailor extension services to local needs.

4. **Kenya:** Kenya's agricultural extension system has undergone significant transformation, moving from a state-led model to a pluralistic approach involving multiple stakeholders, including private entities, NGOs and farmer organizations. The focus has shifted towards market-oriented extension, integrating ICT tools like mobile phones to reach smallholder farmers. The National Agricultural and Rural Inclusive Growth Project (NARIGP) supports community-driven approaches to extension, emphasizing capacity building and sustainable practices.
5. **Australia:** Australia's agricultural extension services have evolved from publicly funded models to a mixed approach that includes public, private and community-based organizations. The emphasis is on participatory approaches, innovation and partnerships with private agribusinesses and research institutions. The Australian Government's Department of Agriculture, Fisheries and Forestry supports programs like the Rural Research and Development Corporations (RDCs), which fund Research, Development and Extension (RDE) activities across various agricultural sectors.
6. **China:** China's extension system is predominantly state-led, with significant involvement from the Ministry of Agriculture and Rural Affairs (MARA). The country's policy emphasizes modern agricultural techniques, digital extension services and a strong focus on food security. Recent reforms have aimed to improve efficiency, farmer participation and market orientation, with increasing collaboration with the private sector and international organizations.

Global experiences with extension policy demonstrate a trend towards decentralization, privatization and the integration of ICT tools to enhance the effectiveness and reach of extension services. However, challenges such as inadequate funding, limited access for marginalized communities and coordination among multiple stakeholders remain common across many countries.

Explicit Extension Policy vs. Extension as Part of Agricultural Policy

Agricultural extension services are essential in disseminating knowledge, improving farming practices and increasing productivity. However, the approach to formulating and implementing these services can vary significantly between having an explicit extension policy and integrating extension as a component of broader agricultural policy.

1. Explicit Extension Policy

An **explicit extension policy** is a standalone policy framework dedicated solely to agricultural extension services. It defines the objectives, strategies, resources and institutional arrangements specific to extension activities. This approach often provides clarity on the roles and responsibilities of various stakeholders, funding mechanisms and the delivery methods for extension services.

a) Advantages

- **Focused approach:** An explicit policy ensures that extension services receive dedicated attention, funding and strategic direction, which can lead to more effective implementation and measurable outcomes.
- **Coordination and accountability:** It provides a clear structure for coordination among government agencies, non-governmental organizations and the private sector, enhancing accountability and transparency.

b) Examples

- **Uganda's National Agricultural Advisory Services (NAADS):** Uganda's explicit extension policy focuses on decentralized, demand-driven services. The NAADS was established as an autonomous body to implement the extension policy, emphasizing farmer empowerment, commercialization and the use of private service providers.
- **Ethiopia's Agricultural Extension Strategy:** Ethiopia has a dedicated agricultural extension strategy that emphasizes capacity building, technology transfer and climate-resilient practices, supported by a network of extension agents and farmer training centers.

2. Extension as Part of Agricultural Policy

In contrast, **extension as part of agricultural policy** integrates extension services into a broader policy framework that covers multiple aspects of agriculture, including production, trade, infrastructure and rural development. This approach treats extension as one component among many others within the overall agricultural development strategy.

a) Advantages

- **Holistic development:** Integrating extension into broader agricultural policies allows for a more comprehensive approach to addressing agricultural challenges, ensuring that extension services are aligned with other sectoral goals like food security, rural livelihoods and environmental sustainability.

- **Resource optimization:** It can leverage synergies across different programs and sectors, leading to more efficient use of resources and avoiding duplication of efforts.

b) Examples

- **India's National Mission on Agricultural Extension and Technology (NMAET):** While not a standalone extension policy, NMAET is part of the broader agricultural policy framework aimed at improving productivity and sustainability through a combination of extension services, technology dissemination and capacity building.
- **China's Agricultural policy reforms:** China incorporates extension services within its wider agricultural policy framework, focusing on modernizing agriculture, improving productivity and ensuring food security through state-led extension services and market-driven approaches .

The choice between an explicit extension policy and integrating extension into broader agricultural policy depends on a country's specific context, including its agricultural landscape, governance structure and development goals. An explicit extension policy offers a focused and targeted approach, while integration within a broader policy framework can provide a more holistic and resource-efficient strategy.

Challenges in Policy Implementation: Capacity, Financial Resources, Ownership and Stakeholder Consultations

Implementing agricultural policies, including those related to extension services, often encounters multiple challenges. Key obstacles include a lack of institutional capacities, inadequate financial resources, insufficient ownership of the policies by local actors and a lack of stakeholder consultations. Each of these challenges affects the effectiveness and sustainability of policy outcomes.

1. Lack of Capacities

A significant challenge in policy implementation is the limited capacity of institutions and personnel responsible for delivering agricultural extension services. This can include a shortage of trained extension workers, inadequate skills in modern agricultural practices and limited access to technology and information.

Impact

- The lack of capacities often leads to suboptimal delivery of extension services, reduced reach among farmers and weak monitoring and evaluation systems. It hampers the ability of institutions to adapt to changing agricultural contexts, such as climate change or market fluctuations.
- For example, in many developing countries, there are not enough trained extension agents to cover all farming communities, which reduces the effectiveness of agricultural policies and limits farmers' access to critical information and support.

2. Inadequate Financial Resources

Insufficient funding is another common challenge that affects the implementation of agricultural policies. Financial constraints can lead to reduced operational capacity, lack of investment in infrastructure and technology and inadequate compensation for extension workers.

Impact

- Limited financial resources can result in a shortage of necessary tools and materials for extension activities, such as vehicles for field visits, training materials and ICT tools. This diminishes the ability of extension services to reach remote or underserved communities effectively.
- Countries like Malawi have faced challenges in implementing their agricultural extension policies due to budgetary constraints, leading to reduced program effectiveness and scalability.

3. Lack of Ownership

Ownership of policies by local actors, including government agencies, local communities and extension workers, is crucial for successful implementation. When stakeholders do not feel a sense of ownership, policies may be implemented half-heartedly or ignored altogether.

Impact

- Lack of ownership often leads to weak commitment from local governments and communities, resulting in poor policy execution and sustainability. It can also cause a disconnect between policy objectives and local needs, reducing the overall effectiveness of the intervention.
- In some African countries, agricultural policies have failed to achieve desired outcomes because they were perceived as externally imposed, lacking alignment with local priorities and farmer needs.

4. Lack of Stakeholder Consultations

The lack of adequate consultation with stakeholders—such as farmers, local governments, NGOs and private sector actors—can undermine the effectiveness of policy implementation. Policies formulated without the input of those directly affected may fail to address real challenges or leverage local knowledge and resources.

Impact

- When policies are developed without inclusive consultations, they risk being misaligned with the needs and capacities of local communities, leading to resistance, non-compliance or failure to achieve intended outcomes.
- For instance, in many regions, top-down approaches to policy formulation have led to the neglect of smallholder farmers' perspectives, resulting in policies that are not adequately targeted or prioritized for those they are meant to serve.

Addressing these challenges requires a comprehensive strategy that includes capacity building, sustainable financial planning, fostering local ownership and ensuring broad-based consultations during policy formulation and implementation. Effective policies are those that consider local contexts, are adequately funded and involve all relevant stakeholders in their design and execution.

Strengthening Capacities in Extension to Influence Policies: Efforts by the Global Forum for Rural Advisory Services (GFRAS)

The Global Forum for Rural Advisory Services (GFRAS) is a leading international organization focused on enhancing the effectiveness and reach of Rural Advisory Services (RAS) globally. One of its key areas of work is strengthening the capacities of extension professionals and organizations to influence agricultural and rural development policies. GFRAS aims to bridge the gap between research, policy and practice through various initiatives, including the development of a policy compendium, specialized training modules and capacity-building programs.

1. Policy Compendium

The GFRAS policy Compendium is a comprehensive resource designed to support extension and advisory service providers in understanding, developing and advocating for effective agricultural policies. The compendium offers a range of policy briefs, guidelines and case studies that highlight best practices and successful examples of policy advocacy in different contexts.

Impact

- The compendium serves as a valuable tool for extension agents and organizations to better understand the policy environment and identify entry points for advocacy. It provides evidence-based recommendations and strategies to effectively engage with policymakers and stakeholders at local, national and international levels.
- By using the compendium, extension professionals can enhance their ability to articulate the needs and priorities of rural communities, thereby influencing policy decisions that support sustainable agricultural development.

2. Training Modules for Policy Advocacy

GFRAS has developed a series of training modules to build the capacity of extension professionals and organizations in policy advocacy. These modules cover key topics such as understanding the policy process, stakeholder analysis, communication strategies and negotiation skills.

Impact

- The training modules are designed to be practical and interactive, enabling participants to learn through real-world scenarios, role-playing and case studies. This approach helps extension professionals develop the skills necessary to effectively advocate for policy changes that promote inclusive and sustainable agricultural development.
- The training also focuses on building networks and partnerships among extension actors, which is crucial for collective advocacy efforts and amplifying the voices of rural communities in policy dialogues.

3. Training to Increase Capacity to Influence Policies

In addition to developing training modules, GFRAS conducts regular capacity-building workshops and training sessions aimed at strengthening the ability of rural advisory service providers to engage in policy advocacy. These training programs are often conducted in collaboration with regional and national networks, such as the African Forum for Agricultural Advisory Services (AFAAS) and the Asia-Pacific Islands Rural Advisory Services (APIRAS).

Impact

- The training sessions provide extension professionals with the tools and techniques needed to effectively communicate with policymakers, present evidence-based arguments and engage in constructive policy dialogues.

- Participants learn to identify key policy issues, develop advocacy strategies and build alliances with other stakeholders, including farmers, NGOs and private sector actors. This holistic approach helps extension providers become more influential in shaping policies that support rural development.

GFRAS's efforts in strengthening capacities for policy advocacy are crucial for empowering rural advisory services to play a more active role in shaping agricultural policies. By providing resources like the policy compendium, developing specialized training modules and conducting capacity-building programs, GFRAS helps extension professionals and organizations become more effective advocates for sustainable and inclusive agricultural development.

References

Agricultural Extension Service. (1978). Agricultural extension in Japan. Tokyo: Japan Agricultural Extension and Development Association.

Alexandratos, N. (1995). World agriculture: Towards 2010,an FAO study.West Sussex, England: FAO and John Wiley & Sons.

Amanda nieweler (2022) Importance of Policies and Procedures in an Organization, Blog, Whistle Blower Security. Study of the agricultural extension experiences in the Republic of Korea. Rome: FAO.

Anderson, J. E. (2010). Public Policymaking: An Introduction. Cengage Learning.

Anderson, J. R. and Feder, G. (2007). "Agricultural Extension." In R. Evenson and P. Pingali (Eds.), Handbook of Agricultural Economics, 3: 2343-2378.

Asian Productivity Organization (APO). (1994). Agricultural extension systems in Asia and the Pacific. Tokyo: Asian Productivity Organization.

Bardach, E. and Patashnik, E. M. (2020). A Practical Guide for Policy Analysis: The Eightfold Path to More Effective Problem Solving (6th ed.). CQ Press.

Bauld, L. and McGill, E. (2008). Improving the Quality of Policy Research: A Guide for Researchers and Policy Makers, Policy Press.

Beauchamp, T. L. and Childress, J. F. (2019). Principles of biomedical ethics (8th ed.). Oxford University Press.

Bertot, J. C., Jaeger, P. T. and Grimes, J. M. (2012). "Using ICTs to promote more inclusive policy processes." Government Information Quarterly, 29(3): 394-400.

Birkland, T. A. (2020). An Introduction to the Policy Process: Theories, Concepts and Models of Public Policy Making (5th ed.). Routledge.

Birner, R., Davis, K., Pender, J., Nkonya, E., Anandajayasekeram, P., Ekboir, J. and Mbabu, A. (2009). From Best Practice to Best Fit: A Framework for Analyzing Agricultural Advisory Services Worldwide. Journal of Agricultural Education and Extension, 15(4): 341-355.

Boardman, A. E., Greenberg, D. H., Vining, A. R. and Weimer, D. L. (2018). Cost-Benefit Analysis: Concepts and Practice (5th ed.). Cambridge University Press.

Brazilian Agricultural Research Corporation (EMBRAPA) (2023). Agricultural Extension in Brazil.

Brunner, R. D. and Steelman, T. (2005). A Guide to Collaborative Policy Making, Routledge.

Cairney, P. (2016). The Politics of Evidence-Based Policy Making, Palgrave Macmillan.

Cartwright, N. and Hardie, J. (2012). Evidence-Based Policy: A Practical Guide to Doing It Better, Oxford University Press.

Chambers, R. (1994). The origins and practice of Participatory Rural Appraisal, world development, 22(7): 953-969.

Chung, Yong-Bok, et al. (1985). Agricultural extension services in Korea.Seodun-dong, Suwon, Republic of Korea: Rural Development Administration.

Cohen, J. E. (2011). The Boundaries of the policy process: Media, policy and politics, Routledge.

Coutts, J. (1994). Process, paper policy and practice: A case study of the introduction of a formal extension policy in Queensland, Australia, 1987-1994. Den Haag: Koninklijke Bibliotheek.

Crawford, B.A., Kramer, D.W. and Hinton, J.W. (2016). Comparing student and professional responses toward advocacy in science.Hum Dimens Wildlife. 21, 361-370. chrome://external-file/GFRAS_Module15-RAS_Policy_Advocacy-Man ual.pdf

Creswell, J. W. and Creswell, J. D. (2017). Research Design: Qualitative, Quantitative and Mixed Methods Approaches (5th ed.), SAGE Publications.

Dunn, W. N. (2017). Public Policy Analysis: An Integrated Approach (6th ed.), Routledge.

FAO. (1990). Women in agricultural development: FAO's plan of action. Rome: FAO.

FAO. (1991). International directory of agricultural extension organizations. Rome: FAO.

FAO and Ministry of Agriculture, the Netherlands. (1991). FAO/Netherlands Conference on Agriculture and the Environment: The den Bosch Declaration and Agenda for Action on Sustainable Agriculture and Rural Development - Report of the Conference. Rome: FAO and the Ministry of Agriculture, Nature Management and Fisheries of the Netherlands.

FAO and Ministry of Agriculture, the Netherlands. (1991). FAO/Netherlands Conference on Agriculture and the Environment: The den Bosch Declaration and Agenda for Action on Sustainable Agriculture and Rural Development - Report of the Conference. Rome: FAO and the Ministry of Agriculture, Nature Management and Fisheries of the Netherlands.

Federal Extension Service (FES). (;.... 1974). Extension international exchange. Washington, DC: Federal Extension Service, U.S. Dept. of Agriculture.

Food and Agriculture Organization of the United Nations (2014). Agricultural Extension, Rural Development and the Food Security Challenge. Rome.

Global Forum for Rural Advisory Services (GFRAS) (2021). Training Modules for Policy Advocacy in Agricultural Extension and Advisory Services.

Hojnacki, M. and Kimball, D. C. (1998). "Organized Interests and the Politics of Advocacy: The Influence of Advocacy Groups on Public Policy." Political Research Quarterly, 51(2): 387-410.

https://advocacyguide.icpolicyadvocacy.org/21-defining-policy-advocacy

https://advocacyguide.icpolicyadvocacy.org/22-different-approaches-to-policy-advocacy

https://blog.whistleblowersecurity.com/blog/importance-of-policies-and-procedures-in-an organization

https://en.wikipedia.org/wiki/Policy_advocacy

https://faolex.fao.org/docs/pdf/bgd147059.pdf am361e.pdf

https://iwrmactionhub.org/learn/iwrm-tools/behaviour-communication-change

https://main.mohfw.gov.in/sites/default/files/17563256478856633221.pdf

https://straydoginstitute.org/agricultural-policy/

https://www.fao.org/

https://www.linkedin.com/pulse/classification-policies-understanding-different-types-ram-m

https://www.lse.ac.uk/social-policy/about-us/What-is-soc ial-policy

https://www.sciencedirect.com/topics/earth-and-planetary-sciences/ag ricultural-policy

https://www.studocu.com/ph/document/palawan-state-university/agricultural economics/chapter-1-intro-to-ag-policy/41862999

https://www.zambianguardian.com/the-4-types-of-policy/

International Centre for policy advocacy (ICPA). Making Research evidence matter- a guide to policy advocacy in transition countries (2014). Different approaches to policy advocacy. Icpolicyadvocacy.org (Retrieved on 02/05/2023).

Jones, G. (1986). Investing in rural extension: Strategies and goals. London: Elsevier Applied Science Publishers.

Kelsey, L., & Hearne, C. (1963). Cooperative extension work. Ithaca, NY: Comstock Publishing Associates of Cornell University Press.

Kingdon, J. W. (2011). Agendas, Alternatives and Public Policies, Longman.

Klijn, E.-H. and Koppenjan, J. (2000). "Public management and policy networks: Foundations of a network approach to public

Ministry of Agriculture, Livestock, Fisheries and Cooperatives, Kenya (2023). National Agricultural and Rural Inclusive Growth Project (NARIGP).

Ministry of Agriculture and Rural Affairs, China (2023). Agricultural Extension Policy Reforms.

Murdock, G. and Golding, P. (2005). "Global Media and Communication Policy: Theories, Practices and Future Directions." Journal of Communication, 55(4): 575-594.

Mwamakamba. S., (2016). Policy advocacy for rural advisory services. Global forum for rural advisory services (GFRAS). Pg no 1-69. www.g-fras.org (Retrieved on02/05/2023).

National Agricultural Advisory Services (NAADS), Uganda (2023).

Nutley, S., Morton, S., Jung, T. and Boaz, A. (2010). "Evidence and Policy in Six European Countries: Diverse Approaches and Common Challenges." Evidence and Policy: A Journal of Research, Debate and Practice, 6(2), 131-144.

Peters, B. G. (2018). Advanced Introduction to Public Policy, Edward Elgar Publishing.

Rivera, W and Gustafson, D. (1991). Agricultural extension: Worldwide institutional evolution and forces for change. Amsterdam: Elsevier.

Rogers, E. M. (1995). Diffusion of innovations (4th ed.). New York: Free Press.

Seddon, T. and Kivunja, C. (2016). ICT and Policy Advocacy: New Directions in the Digital Era. Routledge.

Smith, M. J. (2016). Theories of the Policy Process (3rd ed.). Westview Press.

Smith, R. (2016). Strategic Communications: A Guide to Organizational Success, Wiley.

Smith, R. A. (1995). Political Advocacy and Lobbying: A Guide to Influence Strategies, University of Chicago Press.

Start, D. and Hovland, I. (2004). Tools for Policy Impact: A Handbook for Researcher, Overseas Development Institute (ODI).

Stocking, M. (Ed.). (1994). Report of the Expert Consultation on Integrating Environmental and Sustainable Development Themes into Agricultural Education and Extension Programmes. Rome: FAO.

Swanson, B. (Ed.). (1984). Agricultural extension: A reference manual. Rome: FAO The United Nations' Sustainable Development Goals (SDGs) provide a global reference framework that many countries use to shape their agricultural extension policies, aligning them with goals like zero hunger (SDG 2) and sustainable agriculture (SDG 12).

Swanson, B. (Ed.). (1990). Global Consultation on Agricultural Extension: A report. Rome: FAO.

Tapiwa Kapisa (2021) Process of policy formulation. Newsletter, Guardian- The Student Guide Toolkits. Designing an advocacy strategy. http://toolkits.knowledgesuccess.org (Retrieved on 02/05/2023).

Vickie Sigman (2012) Notes on agriculture extension policies with examples from africa (nigeria, malawi, ghana) and asia (bangladesh), International Agriculture and Extension Education Specialist, University of Illinois Consultant to Modernizing Extension and Advisory Services (MEAS).

Weimer, D. L. and Vining, A. R. (2017). Policy Analysis: Concepts and Practice (6th ed.), Routledge.

Weiss, C. H. (1977). "Research for Policy's Sake: The Enlightenment Function of Social Research." Policy Analysis, 3(4): 531.

World @nimal net (2017).What is advocacy strategy. https://worldanimal.net. (Retrieved on (01/05/2023).

Index